Life Happens

Life Happens

Help Your Teenager Get Ready

BARRY ST. CLAIR

Foreword by Josh McDowell

Nashville, Tennessee

Printed in the United States of America

Published by Broadman & Holman Publishers, Nashville, Tennessee
Acquisitions & Development Editor: Janis Whipple
Interior Design: Desktop Miracles, Addison, Texas
Published in association with the literary agency of Alive Communications, Inc.,
1465 Kelly Johnson Blvd., Suite 320, Colorado Springs, CO 80920.

4262-95
0-8054-6295-3

Dewey Decimal Classification: 248.83
Subject Heading: CHRISTIAN LIFE / TEENAGERS—RELIGIOUS LIFE
Library of Congress Card Catalog Number: 96-36514

Library of Congress Cataloging-in-Publication Data

St. Clair, Barry
Life happens : help your teenager get ready / Barry St. Clair
p. cm.
Includes bibliographical references.
Summary: Explains the importance of Christians discovering their destiny and preparing for their future, covering such topics as spiritual resources, motivation, integrity, values, goals, and decision making.
ISBN 0-8054-6295-3 (pbk.)
1. Teenagers—Religious life. 2. Teenagers—Conduct of life. 3. Parent and teenagers—Religious aspects—Christianity. [1. Christian life. 2. Conduct of life.] I. Title.

BV4531.2.S6744 1997
248.8'—dc20 96-36514
CIP

97 98 99 00 01 5 4 3 2

In honor of my parents,
Howard and Kitty St. Clair,
I write this book.

WITH LOVE THEY ENCOURAGED ME to pursue my destiny. Because of them I never doubted that it was special.

From my dad I learned to dream big dreams and then pursue them. From my mom I learned to persevere through the tough times. From them both I learned to turn to the Lord.

They pursued God's special destiny for them in their generation, and they have left me a legacy that has positively encouraged me to pursue God's unique destiny for me in my generation.

And now Carol and I have the privilege of doing the same with our children and they in turn with their children —generation to generation until all know that God has a destiny for them.

Thanks, Mom and Dad, for leaving me a legacy that
pointed to God's destiny for me!

You have made known to me
    the path of life;
you will fill me with joy
    in your presence,
with eternal pleasures
    at your right hand.

PSALM 16:11

Contents

How Am I Going to Get There?

Foreword

EVERY PARENT WANTS THEIR TEENAGERS to discover the answers to life's three most important questions: Who am I? Where am I going? How am I going to get there? About 95 percent of all teenagers cannot answer these three critical questions with conviction. As a parent, your role is to help your teenagers discover their answers to these questions. This doesn't need to strike terror in your heart. Fortunately for you, Barry St. Clair has written *Life Happens: Help Your Teenager Get Ready*. This book gives you the practical tools to work with your teenagers to help them determine God's destiny for their lives.

In a positive, relationship building experience, you can sit down over a Coke or coffee with your teenagers and help them discover their destiny by identifying their personality type, spiritual gifts, abilities and experience, and motivation. They will come to grips with their purpose, values, goals, and use of time. You will find out how to integrate all of this into a "life plan."

By the time you complete the book, not only will you have challenged your teenagers to discover their destiny, but you will have a better handle on yours as well.

To assist you in working with your teenager, Barry has written a book *for your teenager* entitled *Life Happens: Get Ready*. Its fun, to-the-point style will draw your teenager into making all of these discoveries for themselves.

More than anything I've read in a long time, these books will motivate, focus, and direct you and your teenager toward getting ready for life—now!

JOSH MCDOWELL

Acknowledgments

THE TEAM EFFORT ON THIS BOOK MADE IT POSSIBLE.

Jody Graham, thanks for your encouragement to put what I spoke into print.

Beth Wilson and Mark Deaton, I appreciate you for typing my notes and helping me in so many other ways.

To my office staff who covered for me when I was hiding out, especially Susan Nichols and Brad Leeper.

Most of all, thanks to my Carol, who loves me in spite of myself, who never gives up on me, who has sacrificed many hours of time with me so I could complete this project, and who always encourages me to pursue my dreams.

Why Spend Your Time on This Book?

GRADUATION.
College.
Job.
Career.
Lifelong friends.
Marriage partner.
And many other weighty decisions.

In the next five years your teenager will have made most of these life-changing decisions or will be well on the way toward making them. As a parent, that is a scary thought!

Who is Jesus Christ to them?
What kind of personality do they have?
What spiritual gifts do they possess?
What motivates them?
What is their purpose in life?
What do they value?
What are their goals?
How do they make decisions?

Answering these questions *now* will *protect* them from wasting their lives in the future, and will *provide* them with the resources to fulfill their unique and special destiny.

Lloyd's Bank of London followed 100,000 paper clips and observed that only about 2,000 were used to hold papers together. The bank said:

- 14,163 others were bent and twisted during telephone conversations.
- 19,143 were used as chips in card games.
- 7,200 clipped together garments.
- 5,434 became toothpicks or ear scratchers.
- 5,308 were converted into nail cleaners.
- 3,916 cleaned pipes.

The rest, about 25,000, fell ingloriously to the floor and were swept away.

How could something so neatly invented and so useful be so misused and, often, at least, seemingly wasted? As parents, we want to ask ourselves that question about our lives and the lives of our teenagers. Are we picking teeth and cleaning nails when clearly God has made us and our children for something much more?

How to Max Out This Book

THIS BOOK CREATES THE OPPORTUNITY for significant, life-changing discussions with your teenager. It can change you, and *Life Happens: Get Ready,* the companion book, can significantly impact your teenager! These books will help you and your teenager answer three important questions:

Where am I going?
Who am I?
How am I going to get there?

Because of the importance of the answers to those questions, I want you and your teenager to get the most out of this book.

Most students today don't have a focus to their lives. Through this book you can help your teenager overcome that. Together you will *discover your destiny*. Your destiny is that unique purpose for which God created you—both now and in the future. He has a very special plan designed just for you and for your teenager. As you find His design and help your teenager discover his or hers, then both of you will be focused and motivated to pursue your destiny with a passion!

So how do you max out the book?

- *Pray* before each session. This prayer would be a good one: "Lord, help me discover something new about You and me."
- *Work* through the chapter.
  - Read the material.
  - Look up the Bible verses.
  - Think through your answers.
  - Write down the answers.
  - Jot down any questions you have.

Note: You will experience a shift between chapters 4 and 5. The first four chapters build the foundation. The remaining chapters have an intensely practical bent to them.

- *Focus* on the "Get Ready" section. It will help you to see how what you are learning fits into your life.
  - Set aside at least half an hour for each chapter to work on this.
  - Take your time.
  - Think and pray about it. Let God show you who you are.
- *Apply* what you discover that week. Answer the question: "This week how will I use what I learned?"
- *Talk* about what you learned with your teenager and/or some friends.
  - Order the book *Life Happens: Get Ready* for your teenager.
  - Ask if he or she would be willing to meet with you to talk about what both of you are learning.
  - Set a time to get together. Be flexible with this. Flex your schedule to theirs as much as possible. If you miss a week, that's OK. Set the schedule again for the next week.
  - Use the "Funtalk" section of each chapter to guide you in your conversation with your teenager.
  - You, your church's youth leader, or someone else may want to get a parent's group together to discuss the book. That forum will allow you to learn from other parents' experiences. The "Parents Group Discussion" will help you lead that.

Life happens! It's time for you, and your teenager, to *get ready!*

Note to Youth Leaders:

In using *Life Happens!* with your youth group, you can break it down for study—it's really three books in one:

Where Am I going?
Who Am I? and
How Am I Going to Get There?

Where Am I Going?

1 Let's Party

What is your teenager's destiny, and how can he or she get in on it?

Sweet Sixteen! My daughter Katie got breakfast in bed before school. Immediately after school I took Katie to get her driver's license—her rite of passage into adulthood. She drove out of there without hitting one parallel parking cone and with her license. And we made it home without a wreck!

Later that night, seven of her friends arrived to celebrate. And celebrate we did! We drove across Atlanta to the $3 Cafe. (Not as cheap as it sounds!) We ate burgers and drank cokes and watched movie clips on a large screen TV. Then we drove down to see Steve McCoy, DJ for "Star 94." He had taken the challenge to stay up on an Atlanta Braves billboard until the Braves won the pennant. He came down to talk and to wish Katie a happy birthday. That was big!

WHY ARE BIRTHDAYS SO SPECIAL? Physical birth, spiritual birth—both are worth celebrating because both show how special we are. In both we begin the journey toward our true destiny, the specific purpose for which God created us. And in both of these events our children start down the road to their destinies as well.

As parents we must resist the idea that this is so elementary that we can skip it and move on to deeper things. Vince Lombardi, legendary coach of the Green Bay Packers, gathered his players on the first day of practice every season and said, "Gentlemen, this is a football." If this chapter is a review for you or your teenager, use it as an opportunity to embed these essential, core realities deeper into the fabric of your lives.

Our children need to continually review the basics. About 95 percent of the young people in church can't articulate the simple truths of the gospel, much less elaborate on who they are in Christ.

Since we will communicate these essential truths to our teens, we need to have them on the tip of our tongues. Our confidence will help our kids get it more easily. We won't skip these basics for the same reason we don't want people to skip our birthday saying, "We did that last year, why do it again?"

So let's sing "Happy Birthday!" Let's discover our destiny—and our teenagers' destiny! Let's party!

CATCHING A GORGEOUS GLIMPSE

> When I visit my folks in West Virginia, I have a route that I jog out on Old Ingleside Road. I run up the mountain, turn along the ridge to Mt. Horeb Church, and then return. On this particular day it had just stopped raining. As I ran along the ridge I looked to my right just as the sun burst through the clouds. When it headed down over the edge of the mountain, reflecting against the leaves, the brilliancy of the gold, red, and orange was incredible. It stopped me in my tracks. I said out loud, "Lord, that is unbelievably gorgeous. Thank You for letting me get a little glimpse of You."

We have that same sense of awe when we discover our destiny and help our children discover theirs. When we see God's gorgeous picture of who He is, what He is like, and what He has done for us, then that changes everything. That understanding changes especially the way we see ourselves and the way we see the future God has for us.

That gorgeous glimpse of our destiny resounds in the words of the apostle Paul.

> Because of the sacrifice of the Messiah, his blood poured out on the altar of the Cross, we're a free people—free of penalties and punishments chalked up by all our misdeeds. And not just barely free, either. *Abundantly free!* He thought of everything, provided for everything we could possibly need, letting us in on the plans he took such delight in making. He set it all out before us in Christ, a long-range plan in which everything would be brought together and summed up in him, everything in deepest heaven, everything on planet earth.
>
> It's in Christ that we find out who we are and what we are living for. Long before we first heard of Christ and

> got our hopes up, he had his eye on us, had designs on us for glorious living, part of the overall purpose he is working out in everything and everyone. (Eph. 1:9–12, THE MESSAGE)

Wow! With great delight God eagerly wants to show us our destiny. He centered our destiny around Jesus Christ. We were created to live "in Christ." When we live "in Christ," much more than just pursuing our future life direction is involved—we discover who He is. He is our destiny.

If you read Ephesians 1:1–14 and circle the phrases "in Christ," "in him," and "in the One he loves," you will discover those phrases occur ten times.

God wants us to know that our destiny is "in Christ." But what does that mean?

BACK TO THE FUTURE

Being in Christ is somewhat akin to getting into Dr. Emmett Brown's DeLorean in *Back to the Future*. To get in the time machine and go all the way back to our future "in Christ" is wilder than Marty McFly dating his own mother! But let's hop in and take a ride.

The Past

The Mess Up. From a perfect life to the pits, humankind made a mess out of God's destiny.

At one point in time everything flowed in harmony with God's destiny for the universe (Gen. 1:31). But then Satan, the fallen angel, tempted human beings, who then joined in the rebellion (Gen. 3). That created a gigantic gulf between God and the rest of His creation. The Old Testament showcases people's efforts to find a way back to their destiny, to bridge the gulf between themselves and God. Men and women made laws, offered sacrifices, worshiped idols, and tried doing their own thing—none of which worked.

The Fix Up. These futile attempts to discover their destiny continued until Jesus was born. "But when the time had arrived that was set by God the Father, God sent his Son, born among us of a woman, born under the conditions of the law so that he might redeem those of us who have been kidnapped by the law. Thus we have been set free to experience our rightful heritage" (Gal. 4:4–5, THE MESSAGE).

Jesus went into the blackness of separation from God. He plunged into the gulf until the darkness caused Him to cry out: "My

God, my God, why have you forsaken me?" While Satan and human wickedness did their worst, He endured the cross. Then came the great cry, "It is finished." Now, no rift, no gulf. He pulled it all back together. His was a rescue mission—to redeem us who had been kidnapped. He is the "first-born of all creation"—the ultimate of what human beings can become. Jesus gave us another shot at our destiny.

The Present

The Struggle. Maybe you thought you had to reach your destiny on your own power. For a long time I tried to live the Christian life like these guys I took on a canoe trip.

> The vehicles took us to the end of the road in the Maine woods. The counselors took the canoes off the racks and put three junior high kids under each one to carry them to the water. Three scrawny guys, who already had backpacks and supplies to carry, hauled these canoes over their heads. It would have been one thing to have carried them one hundred yards, but they kept going . . . and going . . . and going. Unlike the Energizer Bunny, they got real tired, real fast. Sweating profusely from carrying the heavy canoes, the hot day, and walking so far, one stumbled over a root. The canoe lurched forward. It rammed the canoe ahead, causing it to ram the next one. Picture kids, canoes, paddles, and gear were scattered all over the trail. Finally they got to the river. They let out a "wahoo" when they dropped the canoes in the water. We put the gear on board, got all the guys, pushed out into the current, and "chilled." The scenery wasn't much different than when we were walking in the woods, but it sure was a lot more enjoyable.

This story illustrates what it means to be "out of Christ." Many people struggle through life carrying the canoe over their heads, exerting incredible effort to get where they're going. The result is exhaustion, frustration, and lives strewn along the trail.

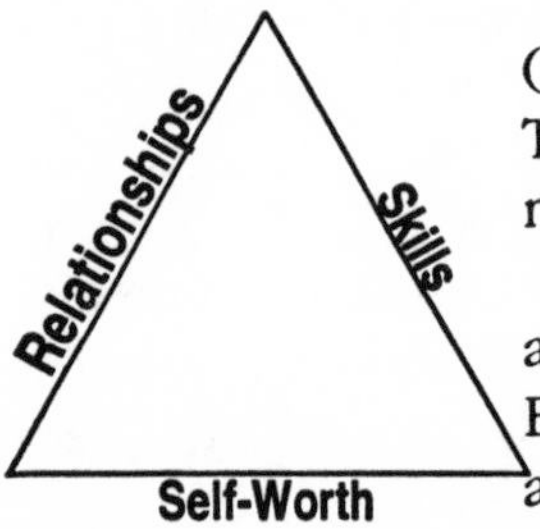

How much better to put the canoe "in (the river of) Christ" and let Him carry us. That's how we and our teens get to our destination—"in Christ."

The Triangle. Let's visualize ourselves, and especially our teenagers, as a triangle. Each side represents a different, but important, aspect of who we are.

In the area of *relationships,* we may have many friends and a great family, but somewhere along the way someone is going to let us down. Facing the wounds our parents may have inflicted, having a friend reject us, dealing with divorce—all of these can cause the relationship side of the triangle to collapse.

In the area of *skills* we may have many talents and abilities; but no matter how talented we are, someone—somewhere—is going to be better than we are. Failing a test, getting injured playing ball, getting fired from a job—all of these and many other circumstances can cause us to question our abilities.

That is why it's so important to build our self-image on the base of the triangle: *self-worth*. Self-worth is based on who we are on the inside, who Christ is in us.

The Prayer. Now, in this present time, each of us can enter into our destiny. We place ourselves "in Christ" by sincerely saying to Him:

> *"Jesus, I open up my life to You. I turn from myself and my sin.*
> *I invite You to come and take control of my life."*

When any person "opens the door" of his or her life, Jesus will come in (Rev. 3:20). At that point a person is "in Christ." It is life's most important decision! You can make it right now, if you have not done so before.

Say this outloud to yourself.

> When Christ died, I died.
> When Christ rose, I rose.
> I am in Christ.
> Christ is in me.
> Now I have a changed identity.

The Future

One day, out there in the future, God is going to bring back together everything that sin and Satan have tried to destroy.

The apostle Paul stated it this way: "And he made known to us the mystery of his will according to his good pleasure, which he purposed in Christ, to be put into effect when the times have reached their fulfillment—to bring all things in heaven and on earth together under one head, even Christ" (Eph. 1:9–10).

In his letter to the church at Philippi, Paul outlines how that is going to happen:

> Therefore God exalted him to the highest place
> and gave him the name that is above every name,
> that at the name of Jesus every knee shall bow,
> in heaven and on earth and under the earth,
> and every tongue confess that Jesus Christ is Lord,
> to the glory of God the Father (Phil. 2:9–11).

Picture a scoreboard. On one side you have the home team's score; on the other you have your opponent's score. Whoever has a higher score at the end of the game wins. The loser cries. The winner celebrates.

In the same way, one day in the future everyone will bow before Jesus as Lord. Some will have placed themselves on the losers' side by living their lives outside of Christ, and they will be heartbroken. Others will have placed themselves "in Christ," and they will celebrate.

Where will you be? Where will your child be? For those of us who have lived out our destiny in Christ—talk about a party!

One day in the future everyone will bow before Jesus as Lord.

Just as Katie's sixteenth birthday celebrated a rite of passage into adulthood, in the same way our spiritual birth is our rite of passage into the incredible depths of who we are in Christ—past, present, and future. More than a formal religious exercise or an emotional experience that passes after a few weeks, it determines who we are. Placing our lives "in Christ" decides our destiny for eternity.

Get Ready

1. If, as you read this chapter, you sensed that you have never placed your life "in Christ," you can do that now. If you prayed the prayer earlier, affirm that decision by thanking God that you are now "in Christ."

    Jesus, thank You for what You did for me at the cross.
    Now I choose to die for myself. Thank You for giving me life when You were raised from the dead.
    I receive You now. I place my life "in Christ" now.
    In Jesus' name. Amen.

2. Celebrate your own birthday! From your discovery in this chapter describe in three sentences what it means to you to be "in Christ."

    ____

    ____

    ____

    ____

    ____

    ____

3. Express your destiny in one sentence.

    ____

    ____

    ____

Helping My Teenager Get Ready

1. Begin to pray daily that your teenager will have a passionate desire to discover his or her destiny in Christ.

   Write your prayer here:

   ____

   ____

   ____

   ____

2. Think creatively about a unique, fresh, fun way to begin to discuss *Life Happens: Get Ready* with your teenager. Consider these options:

   - Going out for breakfast before school or on Saturday morning
   - Meeting after school at a fast food restaurant to get a coke and talk
   - Getting together with a group of your teenager's friends to go through the book
   - Taking a weekend trip to do the first half of the book
   - Taking a weekend trip with a group of parents and their teenagers to discuss the book

   Describe your approach here.

   ____

   ____

   ____

   ____

3. Order the book *Life Happens: Get Ready* for your teen. (You can order from your local Christian bookstore.)
4. Discuss chapter 1 of *Life Happens* with your teenager using the discussion questions in Funtalk.

Funtalk

Use any or all of these questions to stimulate discussion with your teenager about his or her destiny.

Shoot for a twenty-minute discussion. If it goes longer, no problem. But do not drag it out. Keeping it short and interesting will keep your teenager coming back for more.

1. What was the best birthday you ever had? What made it so special? (You tell about your best birthday and what made it special to you.)
2. Let's make a list of what we learned from the chapter on what it means to be "in Christ." I'll tell one thing I learned, then you tell me one. (Refer to the Scriptures and points under the headings on *the past, the present,* and *the future* if necessary, but avoid rehashing the book.)
3. Let's exchange stories about when we entered our destiny "in Christ." Let me tell you what happened to me. Then you can tell me what happened to you.
4. What were the three sentences you wrote to describe what being "in Christ" means to you?
5. Tell me the one sentence you wrote to describe your destiny. Let me tell you mine.
6. Let's pray for both of us that God will fulfill that destiny in us. (You lead in prayer. If your teenager is used to praying aloud, he or she can pray. Otherwise, you lead the prayer.)

Parents' Group Discussion

1. What was the best birthday you ever had? Why was it so special?
2. As a group make a list on the board of what it means to be "in Christ." (Brainstorm this. Keep pushing it back to the Scriptures.)
3. Tell your story about how you entered into your destiny in Christ. Include the three sentences you used to describe what this means to you. (Each person has three minutes.)
4. Tell the sentence you wrote that describes your destiny.
5. What barriers do you think you will encounter in communicating this to your teenagers? (After everyone has talked, see if you can help solve the three biggest ones.)
6. What "unique, fresh, fun" approach will you use to get with your teenager?
7. Pray together for your children by name that they will discover their destiny in Christ.

2 Open the Presents

What spiritual resources does your teenager have, and what can he or she do with them?

As a part of Katie's sixteenth birthday, I took her out to a fancy restaurant. The thirty-ninth floor revolved, offering a panoramic view of Atlanta. After a delicious meal and relaxed conversation, I pulled a small, gift-wrapped box out of my pocket. I told Katie that her mother and I had selected this with special care. She opened it to discover a ruby ring. With it I had attached a note: "You are worth far more than rubies (Prov. 31:10)! We love you. Mom and Dad."

THAT PRESENT EXPRESSED TO KATIE her worth to us. Offered by the hand of a loving father, it spoke volumes about her value as a woman. But more than that, the present showed Katie that her loving heavenly Father sees her as very special and worthwhile.

What is the best gift someone has ever given you? A diamond ring? A new car? Better than the best gifts we have ever received are the ones we possess when we place ourselves "in Christ." Check them out. Open them up for yourself. Then let's help our teenagers open them. These gifts show us and our children how special we are to our heavenly Father. They also provide the spiritual resources that we need to parent God's way and that our kids need to move them toward their destiny.

Present #1—Blessings

Looking at Ephesians 1:3, what blessings has God given us? We have been blessed "with every spiritual blessing in Christ." Jesus, sitting at God's right hand, possesses every resource in the universe. He makes every one of those resources available to us now. To discover our destiny means we learn to tap into the resources of the God of the universe through Jesus Christ.

Lena translates for me when I travel to Ukraine. Her father works two jobs for a total salary of twenty-four dollars a month. Her family has never eaten at a restaurant. She used the forty-five dollars I gave her to buy a warm winter coat for her mile-and-a-half walk every day to catch the train to and from school. Yet she has joy, peace, and unbelievable patience in the midst of an economic system that doesn't work. Lena has ripped open the present of "spiritual blessings."

"Some things a person can work for or discover on his own—certain skills, position, or wealth. But other things are beyond his ability to attain—goodness, humility or peace of mind. 'Spiritual blessings' are those blessings that only God can give."[1]

Those blessings belong to us as believers. What spiritual blessings do you need from God right now? What do your kids need? God will give spiritual blessings to you and your teen-agers in order to fulfill His destiny for you and your children.

PRESENT #2—CHOSEN

Let's unwrap the next present found in Ephesians 1:4. The apostle Paul said, "He chose us in him."

God chose us "before the foundation of the world" (Eph. 1:4, NASB). Since the stars have hung in space, which some say could be billions of years, God has had us in His plans for at least that long!

He chose us "to be holy and blameless in his sight." Are you holy? Are you blameless? What about your teenager? "No way!" you say. Wrong answer.

Imagine your whole life laid out on one of those slides you used in high school biology. Placed under the microscope, what does God see? All the things you have done wrong? Your mistakes? Your messed up relationships? Your sins? No! All He sees when He looks at you is Jesus Christ!

"That doesn't make sense; I sinned, and I still sin," you say. Because you are "in Christ," God doesn't look at that. All He sees is Jesus, holy and blameless in you. Every day He is working to change your attitudes and actions to reflect that.

You are becoming who you already are! So are your kids!

PRESENT #3—ADOPTION

God had only one Son. Everyone else who belongs to Him is adopted. That is why the apostle Paul said, "He predestined us to be adopted as his sons through Jesus Christ" (Eph. 1:5).

All God sees when He looks at you is Jesus Christ!

In the Roman Empire adoption had special significance. The person to be adopted, often out of slavery, went through a ritual of being sold and bought back twice. The third time the person was sold and *not* bought back. Then the adoptive parents signed the papers to legalize the adoption. Finally, the adopted person verbally surrendered all rights to the old family and slavery and took on all the rights of his or her new family and freedom.

Similarly God has adopted us into His family. He promised us that "to all who receive Him He has given the right to become children of God" (John 1:12, NASB).

As God's children we have many privileges. For one, we can call God "our Father." In fact, Jesus encourages us to use the endearing term "Abba," which means "daddy." In a world where good fathers are in short supply, it's wonderful to have the perfect Father. If your relationship with your father is less than the best, then having this kind of relationship with your heavenly Father covers what your earthly father didn't give you. If you struggle with even thinking about God as a Father, I encourage you to imagine yourself sitting on His lap, snuggling up to Him, and letting Him put His arms around you. Let your Father love you.

Becoming part of a family means we become heirs. All of the resources Jesus possessed, we possess now (Rom. 8:17). Read this small sampling out loud and enjoy some of the resources we possess.

- I am loved. (1 John 4:19)
- I am forgiven. (Eph. 1:7)
- I am redeemed. (Gal. 3:13; 1 Pet. 1:18)
- I am changed. (2 Cor. 5:17)
- I am holy. (1 Pet. 1:15–16)
- I am free. (John 8:32)
- I am accepted. (Eph. 1:6)
- I can do all things through Him. (Phil. 4:13)
- I have power. (Acts 1:8)
- I have wisdom. (Col. 2:3)

Knowing we have the privileges of adoption gives us a whole new perspective on our destiny. Not only do we know our family history, rooted in God our Father, but also we possess all of the family resources as "co-heirs with Christ."

You and your children can pursue your destiny knowing your roots and inheritance in God's family.

PRESENT #4—REDEMPTION

If a kidnapper took one of your family members, how would you react? How would you feel? How much would you pay to get that person back?

> Picture a slave market. Chains bind the slaves. Some benevolent benefactor, offering a large sum of money, buys the slave, removing the chains and setting him free.

Humankind had been kidnapped by Satan. We were slaves to sin and selfishness. But Jesus redeemed us (Eph. 1:7). He came into the slave market to buy us back. And He took us out of the slave market forever.

In 1 Peter 1:18–19 we can see what it cost Jesus to do that for us: "For you know that it was not with perishable things such as silver or gold that you were redeemed from the empty way of life handed down to you from your forefathers, but with the precious blood of Christ."

You may say, "I've done some pretty rotten things in my life, and I don't think God can forgive me." Go a step further. Imagine some things even worse than what you have done. Think of the worst crime you could commit. How much forgiveness do you need to take care of it?

> Our family loved to eat at Mother Tucker's. They featured a sixty-dish salad bar, prime rib, a vegetable bar, spareribs on a sideboard, bread, apple dumplings for dessert, and seconds on everything. I would pig out! No matter how much I ate, they always had more.

God's forgiveness comes in quantities like that. He "lavished" it on us (Eph. 1:8). How much forgiveness do you need? If you only need a little, then He will give a little. If you need more, He will give more. If you need mega, He lavishes mega-forgiveness on you. He has taken away all of our sin with mega-forgiveness at the cross. He bought us back with the price of His own blood!

Now nothing from our past, or our teenager's past, holds us back. Destiny here we come!

Present #5—God's Plan

When we play "Charades," we try to figure out the movie, book, or TV program the other team has written down without talking. We give gestures that are clues to help the team guess the answer. When the person starts acting, then everybody on that team yells their guesses until someone gets it or time expires.

People want to know, "What is God's plan for me?" Is it a guessing game? No way. "He made known to us the mystery of his will" (Eph. 1:9). "In Christ" He took all the guesswork out of our future and our children's future as well.

Parents worry about this for their children more than anything else it seems. What a relief to know that not only our future, but theirs as well, will become clear to us at the right time. The mystery is solved!

To gain an understanding of God's plan we must bring every decision, dream, desire, goal, and relationship "under one head, even Christ" (Eph. 1:10). We answer "Yes, Lord," no matter what the question. Our obedience opens the door to the clues of God's will. What areas of your life do you need to bring "under Christ" and say "Yes, Lord"?

He bought us back with the price of His own blood!

What a great gift to know God's will. That certainly builds our confidence that God is moving us and our kids toward our destiny.

Present #6—Acceptance

Being included is a wonderful gift.

My friend Dave Busby had polio and cystic fibrosis as a boy. Since he was always sick, athletics was not his thing. But his older brother had athletic talent. When friends came over to play, Dave would dribble the ball off his gimpy legs. One Saturday morning when he was shooting around with all of his brother's friends, they made fun of him. When it came time to chose sides, he wasn't afraid he would be chosen last; he didn't think he would be chosen at all. His brother was one of the captains. He had first choice. He pointed at his little brother and said, "I choose you, Dave." That made such a profound impact on Dave's life that even now as an adult his view of God is colored by having been included by his brother.

God includes us and our teenagers like that. "And you also were included in Christ when you heard the word of truth" (Eph. 1:13). Like Dave, we aren't included for our abilities, talents, or performance. We are included because we have an Older Brother.

Possibly you have worked hard all of your life to gain approval from family or friends. I talk to many teenagers who feel they can never measure up to their parents' expectations. They feel they have to meet certain performance standards to be included.

- If I achieve success . . .
- If I get good grades . . .
- If I lose weight . . .
- If I make money . . .
- If I go to church . . .

This leads to fear of failure and perfectionistic tendencies. If this goes on long enough and we get rejected enough, it will cause high levels of anxiety and deep depression.

Only one solution exists to combat this fear and anxiety: total, absolute, unconditional acceptance. Jesus is the only One who accepts you like that. When you placed yourself "in Christ," you stepped off the performance treadmill and you stepped into the friendship of One who knows everything about you—good and bad—and still chooses you for His team. Pursuing our family's destiny becomes so much more relaxed when we know we are included on the team and will never be cut.

PRESENT #7—THE HOLY SPIRIT

Did you ever have a letter-writing romance? Guys don't tend to do this well, but girls sure do. When I got one of those letters, no one had to announce its arrival. Everyone could tell by the smell! It reeked of perfume. I don't know which part of the letter I enjoyed more—reading it or smelling it. Before I opened it, one mark on the letter would get me fired up, and it wasn't the postmark. The letter was sealed with a kiss!

When we were marked "in Christ," we were sealed with a kiss, the kiss of the Holy Spirit. "You were marked in him with a seal, the promised Holy Spirit" (Eph. 1:13). A seal is a sign of belonging. The contents in the container belong to the one whose seal is on it. It is a mark that means everything God has promised us now He will deliver.

The Holy Spirit makes sure we get every other gift that God has for us. And there are a bundle of them—character, integrity, love, boldness, sensitivity, power, and communication, to name a few.

Can you fulfill your destiny? Not without the Holy Spirit. Express a prayer asking Him to release His presence and power in you and your teenagers so your family can be and do all He intended.

That ring I gave Katie was a very special present. She wears it with pride. But how small and insignificant it was compared to any one of these presents God has given us "in Christ." With all of these opened presents we have all we will ever need to fulfill God's destiny for us and to guide our families toward God's destiny for them. Let's put the rings on our fingers and wear them!

Get Ready

Think about what you face at home with your spouse and children, at work, or with friends. Relate one specific, practical way you will use each of the seven "presents" in the next week.

1. Blessings ______________________________
2. Chosen ______________________________
3. Adoption ______________________________
4. Redemption ______________________________
5. God's Plan ______________________________
6. Acceptance ______________________________
7. Holy Spirit ______________________________

Helping My Teenager Get Ready

1. Pray that your teenagers will be able to grasp the resources they have "in Christ." Call on the Holy Spirit to reveal that to them.
2. Go through chapter 2 in *Life Happens* with your teenager. Use the following discussion questions.

Funtalk

1. What do you consider the most meaningful present someone has given you? Why was it so valuable to you?

2. Do you think material blessings make it harder or easier to receive and use our spiritual resources? Why do you think so?
3. Let's look at the practical ways we decided to use these seven presents this week. (Talk back and forth about what you wrote down and why. Refer to the chapter if you like.)
4. Close your time asking the Holy Spirit to release His presence and power in you so you can fulfill your destiny. Ask Him to continue to show you the "presents" you have and how to enjoy them and use them.

PARENTS' GROUP DISCUSSION

1. Describe in three sentences your discussion with your teenager last week.
2. What one improvement would you like to see happen this week?
3. Talk about what you consider the most meaningful present someone has given you. Why was it so valuable to you?
4. Share with each other the practical ways you decided to use these seven presents this week. If you have already used some of them, share that too.
5. Discuss the effect material possessions and affluence have on your teenagers that make it harder for them to receive and use spiritual resources. Specifically what can you do about it?
6. These spiritual resources are the key to your success in parenting. You have learned by now that you can't raise teenagers successfully within the limits of your own resources. How do these "presents" affect your parenting?
7. Pray for the Holy Spirit to release His presence and power in you not only to communicate these truths but to live them in front of your kids as well.

3 Take a Trip

What is your teenager's destination, and how does he or she get there?

When I was growing up, my dad liked to take shortcuts on family trips.

"Where are we headed, Dad?"

"Don't worry. We're taking a shortcut."

Every time we got lost. Mom would suggest that we stop and get directions.

"No, I'm sure we are headed in the right direction."

An hour later we would discover that for the last two hours we had been making a beeline to Disney World. But our destination was Washington, D.C.!

IT'S SOMETHING ABOUT DADS. I do exactly the same thing with my family.

Our family knew who we were, but we got confused on our directions. In the same way, we can know our destiny and still get confused about how to arrive at our destination.

Deep inside we know that we have a destination. Certainly we are supposed to go someplace. But all too often we don't know what that destination is. And if *we* don't have a clue, it is no wonder our kids get so confused.

Already we have discovered that our destiny is "in Christ." That is the mode of transportation that gets us down the road to our destination. But where is our road headed? Where are we going?

Don't Take a Wrong Turn

Often our teenagers turn in the wrong direction because they make unwise decisions in the following areas. They see them as disconnected from their destination.

- Dating: Who will I date? Will I ever date?
- Friends: Who will my friends be?
- Sex: Will I have it now or wait until I marry?
- Activities: What will I get involved in at school?
- Job: What kind of job will I get?
- College: Will I go to college? Where will I go?
- Money: How can I make money? How can I make more?

What connects these decisions to the same road? For most teenagers—nothing! Most teenagers make each one of these life-impacting decisions not realizing that they are connected to their destination. Yet for these decisions to make sense they must feed into the freeway that takes our kids to the destination that fulfills their destiny.

Our kids take another wrong turn by viewing God and His plan incorrectly. If they view God as the Celestial Scrooge sitting in heaven with His fifty-pound King James Bible and a big stick, then it's hard to want to follow His plan. Often we think of our future in narrow, negative terms:

- A needle in a haystack. We must constantly search for our destination. Now and then God whispers, "You're getting warmer."
- A wasted life. If we pursue what God wants, then He will send us to "Bogabogaland" and ruin our lives.
- A tightrope. If we make one wrong move, one bad decision, then we will fall off the tightrope and destroy the rest of our lives.
- A computer printout. The "Big Computer in the Sky" will lay out every specific, detailed step of God's will for the rest of our lives. We can't leave home without it. If we do, we will never know God's plan.

To recognize these possible wrong turns before we begin the trip will keep us from wasting time in getting to our destination and keep us on the right road on the way there.

STRAIGHT AHEAD

The flight took me from Kansas City to Chicago, then to Winnipeg, and on to Regina, Canada. From there the van drove an hour and a half down a highway through the wheat fields of western Canada. At one point the van driver pointed down the road and said, "Do you see that blue spot out in the distance?" I could see it easily. Not one building or tree stood between us and that blue roof. He said, "That is where we are going." It took us twenty minutes to get there! That is how far down the road we could see.

God's destination for us is like that. It is way off in the distance, but we can see it and experience it now. Nothing blocks our view. Look out in the distance. You can see it.

Two times in Ephesians 1:1–14 the apostle Paul used the phrase "to the praise of his glory." You can find those in verses 12 and 14. In that phrase we find our destination, both God's future and present plan for us.

Our Destination Is Future

When the apostle Paul used these phrases, he definitely had the future in mind. "Having believed, you were marked in him with a seal, the promised Holy Spirit, who is a deposit guaranteeing our inheritance until the redemption of those who are God's possession —*to the praise of his glory*" (Eph. 1:13–14, author's italics).

We will spend eternity praising His glory. When we see Him face to face, we will be so overwhelmed with the awesomeness of Jesus Christ that we will want to do nothing else but stand in His presence, look at Him in the fullness and completeness of who He is, and praise Him!

Catch a small glimpse of what that will be like:

> Then I heard every creature in heaven and on earth and under the earth and on the sea and all that is in them, singing:
>
> *"To him who sits on the throne and to the Lamb*
> *be praise and honor and glory and power,*
> *for ever and ever!" (Rev. 5:13)*

William Barclay gets us started in that direction: "Here is the great truth that the greatest and highest, and the dearest and the most intimate experience of Christian peace and joy which this world can afford, are only faint foretastes of the joy into which we will one day enter. It is as if God had given us enough to whet our appetites for more, and enough to make us certain that some day He will give us all."[1]

Let this grab you and create a wild enthusiasm about your family's future destination—living "to the praise of his glory."

OUR DESTINATION IS NOW

Since we will spend eternity praising His glory, it makes sense to get in plenty of practice now. Our destination now: to spend every moment of every day for the rest of our lives "living to the praise of his glory."

How does that work? God has given us His Holy Spirit "who is a deposit guaranteeing our inheritance" (Eph. 1:14). When we received Christ, God gave us the Holy Spirit to live in us and to change us so that we reflect Jesus Christ. Because the Holy Spirit lives in us now as a "deposit," we can live to the praise of His glory now.

Over the years how many times did people ask us, "What are you going to be when you grow up?" Depending on our interests at the time, we answered: "A fireman." "A NBA star." "A nurse." "A lawyer."

We are mirrors that reflect who Jesus is.

This phrase "to the praise of his glory" changes our perspective. To begin with, we don't need to wait until we grow up or go to heaven to reach our destination. We can reach it now, today, every day. To "live to the praise of his glory" is a lifestyle, an attitude.

How did the apostle Paul express it in 2 Corinthians 3:18? "But we Christians have no veil over our faces; we can be mirrors that brightly reflect the glory of the Lord. And as the Spirit of the Lord works within us, we become more and more like him" (2 Cor. 3:18, TLB).

When we wake up and look in the mirror (bad hair and all), we need to become keenly aware that all day long we will be mirrors that reflect to other people who Jesus is. They will see His glory through us. They will know the attitudes, actions, and character of Jesus Christ by what they see coming out of our lives.

"Whoa!!!" you say. "That is heavy duty. I can't live up to that. I mess up every day. I am not perfect." So what else is new? The focus here is not on you. You are only a mirror that reflects the Holy Spirit to others. We let the Spirit of the Lord work in us. What does He do in there?

Look at what He gets rid of: "Repetitive, loveless, cheap sex; a stinking accumulation of mental and emotional garbage; frenzied and joyless grabs for happiness; trinket gods; magic-show religion; paranoid loneliness; cutthroat competition; all-consuming-yet-never-satisfied wants; a brutal temper; an impotence to love and be loved; divided homes and divided lives; small-minded and lopsided pursuits; the vicious habit of depersonalizing everyone into a rival; uncontrolled and uncontrollable addictions; ugly parodies of the community" (Gal. 5:19–21, THE MESSAGE).

Jesus will change our thoughts, habits, attitudes, and actions so we behave like Him.

Now look at what He gives you: "Affection for others, exuberance about life, serenity . . . willingness to stick with things, a sense of compassion in the heart, and a conviction that a basic holiness permeates things and people . . . loyal commitments, not needing to force our way in life, able to marshal and direct our energies wisely" (Gal. 5:22–23, THE MESSAGE).

He produces in us the *character* of Jesus Christ. We will be able to honor Christ with our . . .

moral life,
thoughts,
words,
relationships, and
actions.

The Holy Spirit in us provides the resources for us to "become more and more like him." The Holy Spirit takes us straight ahead to our destination: *to live* ***to reflect*** *His glory.*

We don't do that on our own. We don't need to jump higher, try harder, or do better. Instead, we have to call on God's resources to "just do it" in and through us. Over time He is the one who will change our thoughts, our habits, our attitudes, and our actions so that we behave like Jesus Christ.

"In 1492 Columbus Sailed the Ocean Blue . . ."

Because Christopher Columbus took seriously God's destination for his life, and pursued it, we have the privilege of living in America today. Even though you have never read this in a public school text, here is the real story of how he discovered America.

> After his ships had been at sea much longer than anticipated, the crew was ready to mutiny. When they confronted him with turning back, Columbus prayed and then requested three more days. Immediately the wind picked up and the ships moved more swiftly than at any time before. On the evening of the third day they spotted land. He wrote in his journal later:
>
>> "It was the Lord who put it into my mind. (I could feel his hand upon me) the fact that it would be possible to sail from here to the Indies. All who heard of my project rejected it with laughter, ridiculing me. There is no question that the inspiration was from the Holy Spirit, because He comforted me with rays of marvelous inspiration from the Holy Scriptures . . . . I am a most unworthy sinner but I have cried out to the Lord for grace and mercy, and they have covered me completely. I have found the sweetest consolation since I made it my whole purpose to enjoy His marvelous presence. For the execution of the journey to the Indies, I did not make use of intelligence, mathematics or maps. It is simply the fulfillment of [prophecy]."[2]

God's destination—living to reflect His glory—and His resources to get there are the same for us and our teenagers as for Christopher Columbus. Yet our destinations are as uniquely significant as that of Christopher Columbus. Pursue it with a passion!

GET READY

1. Describe some of the shortcuts and wrong turns you have taken that have detained you in reaching your destination.
2. Reflecting on 2 Corinthians 3:18, look at your future and your present to determine what you can do to live to reflect His glory? Write down one practical decision that will move you in that direction.
3. Thinking about the significant way God worked out His destination for Christopher Columbus, what do you think God's unique and significant destination is for you?

Helping My Teenager Get Ready

1. Begin to pray with your child each night that God will fulfill his or her destiny "in Christ" and destination to live to reflect His glory.
2. When you pray with your teenager, read Ephesians 1 together. Share your insights on destiny and destination.
3. Work through chapter 3 of *Life Happens* with your child using Funtalk.

Funtalk

1. Let me tell you the biggest "wrong turn" I ever made in my life. (Transparently share yours.) How would you describe yours?
2. Let's talk about the one decision we made that will help us to live to reflect His glory.
3. After reading the story about Christopher Columbus, what significant way do you think God wants you to live to reflect His glory in you? (Both of you share your hopes and dreams.)
4. Pray for each other that God will give you the strength to live to reflect His glory and to live out your unique destination.

Parents' Group Discussion

1. What is one breakthrough you have had with your teenager since beginning this study? What is one barrier you face?
2. Share a "wrong turn" you have made. Do you feel like that has kept you from pursuing your destination?
3. In the Get Ready section, what practical decision did you make to live to reflect His glory?
4. After reading the Christopher Columbus story, what unique and significant way do you think God wants you to live to reflect His glory in you? In your teenager?
5. Often we watch our children settle for mediocrity. Discuss how you, as a parent, and your church can raise the standard to help your kids make decisions that, instead of reflecting negatively on Christ, can cause them to live in a way that honors Him. Make your discussion creative and practical, concluding with two or three concrete approaches.
6. Pray that God will give your teenagers a desire to live to reflect His glory.

4 Look for the Billboards

How can you help get your teenager where he or she is going and not give up on the way?

When I was a kid, every summer we headed to Florida from West Virginia for our family vacation. Before we crossed the Florida line, billboards advertised "ALL OF THE ORANGE JUICE YOU CAN DRINK FOR 10 CENTS—10 MILES." After driving another mile another sign appeared: "ALL THE ORANGE JUICE YOU CAN DRINK FOR 10 CENTS—9 MILES." Each mile another billboard appeared until, at the end of ten miles, a huge neon sign would scream, "YOU ARE HERE! ALL THE ORANGE JUICE YOU CAN DRINK FOR 10 CENTS." We always stopped at the first juice stand. As a ten-year-old I would drink ten to twelve glasses of juice. One time, after I had guzzled five or six glasses, the owner said, "Son, that's all the orange juice you can drink for ten cents."

AFTER SIGHTING THE FIRST BILLBOARD, I couldn't wait to get to the orange juice stand. I sat on the edge of my seat and read every sign we passed. God has placed some huge, neon billboards along the road to advertise what we and our teenagers need when we get tired, distracted, or stuck on the side of the road in pursuing our destination. Sitting on the edge of our seats, let's read every billboard and take advantage of what it offers.

SEE THE WORLD'S STRONGEST MAN!! (RELY ON GOD'S POWER)

In college I attended a Fellowship of Christian Athletes camp. One day Paul Anderson, the world's strongest man, spoke. He had won the gold medal in the Olympics and held every major weightlifting record in the world. In front of this crowd of seven or eight hundred young athletes he did several feats of strength that caused us to "ooooh" and "ahhhh." But he saved the best until last. He got ten guys from the audience to sit on a large table. Then he got under it and lifted it completely off the ground. That was more weight than anyone had lifted—ever!

"Totally impressed," described me. My mouth hung open. But that was nothing compared to the strength that God infused into Jesus Christ.

The apostle Paul piled one power word on top of another to make the point in Ephesians 1:19–21: "That *power* is like the working of his *mighty strength*, which he exerted in Christ when he raised him from the dead and seated him at his right hand in the heavenly realms, far above all *rule* and *authority, power* and *dominion"* (author's italics).

The writer of Hebrews drove home the point of Jesus' power even more dramatically in the way he described Jesus:

> "The Son is the radiance of God's glory and the exact representation of his being, sustaining all things by his powerful word. After he had provided purification for sins, he sat down at the right hand of the Majesty in heaven" (Heb. 1:3).

"So what?" you say. "I already know that God is powerful and Jesus is strong." Yes, but Paul said this power is "for us" (Eph. 1:19).

"But I don't feel very powerful or strong," you say. "Most of the time I feel like a spiritual wimp."

That's OK because God's power flows more freely in our weakness (2 Cor. 12:9). When we realize how weak we are, then the power of Christ is released through us. Look at 2 Peter 1:3–4 to discover what the power of Christ gives us:

> "For as you know him better, he will give you, through his great power, everything you need for living a truly good life: he even shares his own glory and his own goodness with us! And by that same mighty power he has given us all the other rich and wonderful blessings he promised; for instance, the promise to save us from the lust and rottenness all around us, and to give us his own character" (TLB).

When we rely totally on His power, not our own, then we have what we need to live to reflect His glory!

Now that we have the power, let's drive on down to the next billboard.

Get a Free Gift!!
(Receive God's Grace)

Not one to turn down anything free, if I see a billboard advertising a free gift, I get excited.

All of us feel spiritually weak, and for good reason. According to Ephesians 2:1–3, before we knew Christ we were "dead in [our] trespasses and sins" (v. 1, NASB), we "followed [in] the ways of this world and of the ruler of the kingdom of the air" (Satan, v. 2), and we gratified "the cravings of our sinful nature and [followed] its desires and thoughts" (v. 3). That's worse than weak. Try dead!

Sin did that to us. Sin has left us with

- deep longings—pain in our hearts because of the disappointments of what other people have done to us.
- wrong strategies—our selfishness that tries to satisfy our deepest desires.[1]

To get rid of these deep longings and wrong strategies God has given us three free gifts according to Ephesians 2:5–6.

- Gift 1—He has "made us alive with Christ, even when we were dead in [sin]" (v. 5). We have moved from death to life.
- Gift 2—He has "raised us up [out of sin and death] with Christ" (v. 6). We have the life of Christ living in us.
- Gift 3—He has "seated us with him in the heavenly realms" —the place of power (v. 6). We have all of his power available to us to change our motives, desires, and actions.

Those gifts come to us as a result of His grace (vv. 5, 7–8).

We can begin to get the picture of what a big deal grace is with this definition: "God's supernatural ability in you through the cross and the resurrection."

To finish the picture, drop in these illustrations.

A Credit Card

The bank calls to tell you that they have a credit card for you that has unlimited spending, which unlike our credit cards, you never have to repay. But you tell them you don't want it.

No card is like no grace. You miss out on the unlimited resources that God has made available to you in Christ. But we get to cash in on God's grace.

A Car

On a hot summer day your car runs out of gas. Cars zoom by. You push the car until you get to a hill. Someone offers to help. And you refuse: "No, I always drive it without gas."

No gas is like no grace. We can try hard to live for God, but it is impossible. You have plenty of power under the hood, but no fuel to crank it into action. Yet when we pour in the fuel of grace, which we already have available, we will have more than enough power.

Don't get stuck on the side of the road, saying, "I can't . . . . I don't . . . . I never have . . . ." NO! Receive God's gift of grace within you and move along to the next billboard.

LIVE IN YOUR DREAM HOUSE!! (RECONCILE YOUR RELATIONSHIPS)

Very middle class. That describes the house I grew up in on Hale Avenue. But my parents had a dream. They bought some property that nobody wanted because it had some "undesirable elements." With almost all their savings they bought "the Hill"—about sixty acres that overlooked our town. With "sweat equity" they built a beautiful house with a fantastic view.

To live to reflect His glory we must move into God's dream house. Look at how Paul described it in Ephesians 2:19–22.

> "You are no longer strangers or outsiders. You *belong* here, with as much right to the name Christian as anyone. God is building a home. He's using us all—irrespective of how we got here—in what he is building. He used the apostles and prophets for the foundation. Now he's using you, fitting you in brick by brick, stone by stone, with Christ Jesus as the cornerstone that holds all the parts together. We see it taking shape day after day—a holy temple built by God, all of us built into it, a temple in which God is quite at home" (THE MESSAGE, author's emphasis).

God has designed us to live together in unity. We should function as one brick fitting perfectly with the others. Bricks don't yell,

- "I don't like you."
- "I'm the best brick."
- "I want to be the first brick."

We could solve most problems in the church if we handled our relationships God's way.

If you have wronged someone, Jesus told us what to do. He said that if you come to church to worship and realize that your brother has something against you, "first go and be reconciled to your brother; then come and offer your gift" (Matt. 5:23–24). Can you say with confidence, "I have no barriers in any relationships because of something I have done to harm that relationship"? Have you asked forgiveness of people who have something against you?

If someone has wronged you, again Jesus gave us instructions. He said, "If your brother sins against you, go and show him his fault" (Matt. 18:15). Do you hold a grudge or have resentment toward another person?

You can't confront the other person about what he or she did to you until you release the anger you have. You can't do that honestly if you harbor bitterness over what that person did to you. So you must get the plank out of your eye (your anger) before you try to get the speck out of your brother's eye (his hurtful action) (Matt. 7:3).

Is there anyone toward whom you have anger, resentment, or bitterness?

Unity is God's "dream house." We help build it when we live in unity in our relationships. Then the world will look at us, like it did the early church, and say, "Look how they love each other!"

Now all of us together can travel down the highway to the next billboard.

Solve the Mystery (Relate Christ to Others)

The Great Airport Mystery, The Sinister Signpost, The House on the Cliff. I read every one of the Hardy Boys mysteries, secretly wishing that I had their ability to find clues and courage to solve the mystery.

Now I, along with you, get to fulfill all of our mystery-solving fantasies. In fact, we are key components in solving the greatest mystery of all time. What is it? "The mystery is that people who have never heard of God and those who have heard of him all their lives . . . stand on the same ground before God. They get the same offer, same help, same promises in Christ Jesus. This is my life work: helping people understand and respond to this message" (Eph. 3:6–7, The Message).

We have the incredible privilege of being detectives for the gospel. We get to find the people who have never heard the message of Christ, search for the clue(s) that reveal the empty places in their lives, and then show them how they can fill that "God-shaped vacuum" with the life-changing solution of Jesus Christ.

Most Christians feel awkward, ill-equipped, and uncomfortable as "detectives for the gospel." But it doesn't have to be that way. You can use these practical tools and help your teenager use them too.

- *Verbally identify with Jesus Christ.* Let people around you know that you love and follow Him.
- *Ask someone to show you how to communicate Christ.* A helpful tool is the book *Giving Away Your Faith*. (See page 178 for ordering information.)
- *Pray for three friends who need Christ.* Ask God to get them ready to receive Him.
- *Boldly tell one of your friends your story about Jesus.* Step out of your comfort zone and talk about Him.

God's desire is that we take with us as many people as possible as we pursue our destination of living to reflect His glory.

Along "life's road" it's easy to get tired. As we make the journey to live to reflect His glory these billboards will encourage us, and our teenagers, to stop and get refueled, reenergized, and refreshed along the way.

GET READY

Stop at each billboard exit and pick up the resources that will help you to live to reflect His glory.

- To release God's power I need to . . . (see Eph. 1:19–21).

- To rely on God's grace I need to . . . (see Eph. 2:1–6).

- To reconcile my relationships I need to . . . (see Eph. 2:19–22).

- To relate Christ to unbelievers I need to . . . (see Eph. 3:6–7).

Helping My Teenager Get Ready

1. Each night when you pray with your teenager, read one of the Ephesians' passages and then pick up one billboard resource to help you in living to reflect His glory. ("Lord, tonight I release your power. In order to do that I know I need to . . .")
2. Work through chapter 4 of *Life Happens* with your teenager using Funtalk.

Funtalk

1. Let's think back over the last four sessions and come up with the one thing that has helped us the most and why.
2. Let's share the one way we can use what we discovered from each of the four billboards.
3. Of the four billboards, which one was most important to you? Why?
4. Let's pray for each other that we will rely on God's resources rather than our own, especially with our family and friends.

Parents' Group Discussion

1. Personally, what have you learned about your destiny in Christ and your destination—living to reflect His glory—over the last four weeks?
2. What indication do you have that your teenager has grasped destiny and destination? (If they have not grasped it totally, don't worry because it will come up again and again during the remaining weeks.)
3. Talk about the positives and negatives of your prayer times with your teenager.
4. What resources did you pick up at each of the billboards that will help you live to reflect His glory? Be specific.
5. How have the sessions of the last four weeks changed your perspective on how you parent your children? Give one concrete example.
6. Pray for each other and for your kids that instead of relying on your own resources all of you will rely on God's resources to parent and to live for Christ.

Who Am I?

5 Vote for Yourself

What is your teenager's personality, and how can he or she enjoy it?

Almost every high school in America has the seniors vote on senior superlatives. Best Dressed. Cutest Couple. Friendliest. Most Popular. Most Likely to Succeed. Every school has its own list. Some vote in the negative: Worst Dressed. Biggest Nerd.

One year later we see the gross inaccuracy. The Cutest Couple broke up and both go with someone else. Most Popular lives alone in the mountains. Most Likely to Succeed never made it out of summer school. The end results are understandable. After all, it's only a popularity contest.

To me the most intriguing senior superlative is Best Personality. What does that mean? Does everyone else have a mediocre personality? Does someone qualify as Worst Personality?

THE TRUTH IS THAT EVERYONE DOES have a personality, and that personality is best for him or her. That's where the problem lies. We think that if we, or our teenagers, don't have a certain personality, then we got cheated.

The first time I took a personality test, I loved it! I didn't have to take it for a grade! About halfway through, it dawned on me that everyone is unique. I remembered thinking, "What a dull world we would live in if everyone had the same kind of personality." For the first time I realized that my personality is totally unique from everyone else's. In God's incredible creativity, He fashioned each of us into a totally unique individual, completely different from any other person.

The psalmist expressed that uniqueness beautifully in Psalm 139:13–14. What do you think the psalm says about your unique personality?

For you created my inmost being;
you knit me together in my mother's womb.
I praise you because I am fearfully and wonderfully
made,
your works are wonderful, I know that full well.

Because of each individual's total uniqueness, all of us can vote ourselves Best Personality. As parents, when we understand our unique personality, we will gain insight into why we respond the way we do. Not only will we understand and appreciate ourselves more, we will understand and appreciate our spouses and our children more. Many of the traits that attract us or repel us are found in the arena of personality. That very personality will be a major instrument God will use to move us and our kids toward His destiny for us.

KNOW THYSELF

Socrates said it well, "Know thyself." And we need to, but not for the reasons most people pursue knowing themselves. Our culture is saturated with self-actualization, self-improvement, self-help, and self-everything else. The dominant word in the last sentence gives us a clue as to what the problem is. Understanding our personality for selfish reasons has very little value.

Jesus put the issue of knowing ourselves on a higher plane. He said, "Love the Lord your *God* with all your heart and . . . love your *neighbor* as *yourself*" (author's italics). As we discover the infinite and unique personality of God, we will learn to love Him. Out of that love relationship we will love our neighbors. With a healthy love for God and others, we will have the ability to love our ourselves.

THE HEART OF THE MATTER

The Hebrew people used the word *heart* to define personality. For example, the writer of Proverbs said, "Keep your heart with all vigilance, for from it flow the springs of life" (Prov. 4:23, NRSV).

Out of our personality, "heart," flows life. Therefore, we need to guard our hearts. Don't let anyone "stomp that sucker flat," as Lewis Grizzard would say. This has particular relevance with our teenagers' friendships and dating relationships. One of our major responsibilities is to help our children build a fence around their hearts so they don't give it away to the wrong people or so others don't steal it from them. We need to help them reserve it for God Himself and for that special person with whom they will spend their lives.

The ancient Greeks divided the heart (personality) into several compartments. Note the ones in 1 Thessalonians 5:23: "May your whole spirit, soul and body be kept blameless at the coming of our Lord Jesus Christ."

The "body," our physical makeup—hair, ears, eyes, arms, and legs—expresses the outward, exposed dimension of our personality. The "spirit" connects to that deep inner self that has the capacity to relate to God. The spirit is what Blaise Pascal had in mind with his famous quote: "There is a God-shaped vacuum in the heart of every man that cannot be filled by any created thing, but only by God the Creator, made known through Jesus Christ." The "soul" (personality) connects the body and the spirit, the natural and the supernatural. This bridge has three unique components:

- emotions—our feelings
- mind—our thoughts
- will—our decisions

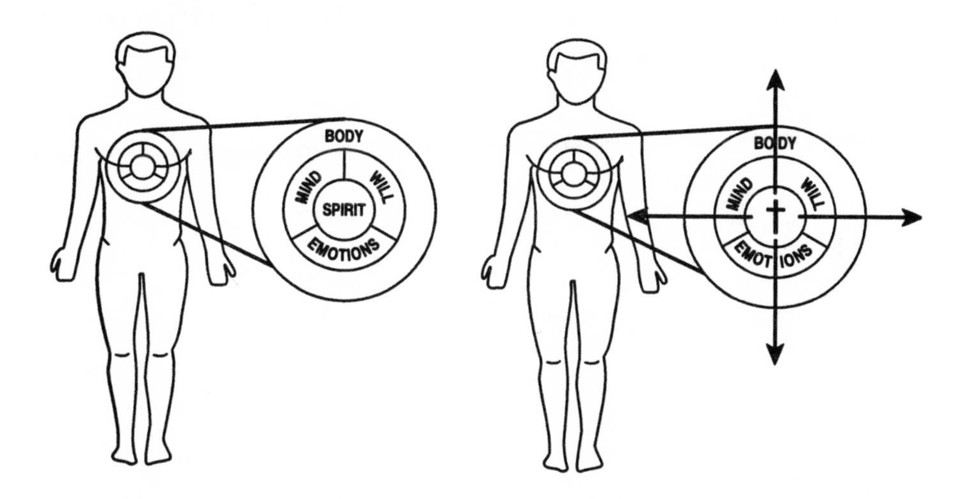

Our entire personality must be transformed because of the adverse impact of sin. That happens as we surrender our spirit to the Holy Spirit. Christ replaces self at the very heart of our personality. We are still ourselves, but Christ is in control of our spirit. Then "Christ in you" begins the process of changing our mind, will, and emotions—how we think, feel, and act. Eventually those changes are expressed through our body. At that point we are moving toward our destination, living to reflect His glory.

Personality Plus

In 2400 B.C. Hippocrates, the famous philosopher/physician, identified four basic personality types. Hippocrates gave names to the temperaments that were suggested by the liquids he thought were the cause: the Sanguine—blood, Choleric—yellow bile, Melancholy —black bile, and Phlegmatic—phlegm. To him, these suggested the lively, active, black, and slow temperaments.[1]

As we discover the four personality types, follow these ground rules.

- No one person is totally a single personality type. We are all a combination to varying degrees.
- These four personality types are broad generalizations with each one having a variety of subpatterns that reveal each person's uniqueness.
- One personality type is not better or worse than another one. Each one has strengths and weaknesses.
- We must resist the temptation to analyze, then stereotype our family and friends. Later on you can help them discover these things for themselves.
- In prayer, ask God to show you more about your personality.

CHOLERIC
(THE DOER)

Doer
Dominant
Directive
Driver
Dynamic
Determined
Developer

Motivated by:

Challenges, projects, results, and the freedom to act

Goal:

To challenge the status quo by controlling the environment and overcoming the opposition in order to achieve the desired results

Strengths and Weaknesses:

STRENGTHS	WEAKNESSES
• Overcomer	• Controversial
• Visionary	• Oblivious to risks, facts
• Decisive	• Overbearing
• Goal oriented	• Impatient
• Persistent	• Inflexible, unyielding
• Initiating	• Dictatorial
• Confident	• Braggart
• Assertive	• Blunt
• Competitive	• Abrasive
• Authoritative	• Demanding
• Independent	• Refuses help
• Results oriented	• Insensitive
• Leader	• Bossy
• Active	• Restless, workaholic
• Delegates	• Manipulative

Best Environment:

- Challenging project
- Variety in schedule and opportunities
- Freedom from control and detail

Biggest Fear:

Incompetence, being taken advantage of

Reaction to Stress:

Takes control

Suggestions for Personal Growth:

- Express empathy and emotion.
- Learn to listen.
- Relax and enjoy life.
- Be honest about weaknesses.
- Say, "I was wrong."
- Give in to others.
- Practice patience.
- Don't brag or say, "I told you so."

To determine if your personality is choleric, take the survey at the end of the chapter. If this is your personality, then intensely pursue God's vision for you. Submit your plans to Him, and pursue them with love and sensitivity. Allow yourself to be "crucified with Christ" daily so that you go after goals that are God's goals and not your own. Then God will help you overcome your weaknesses and will use you to impact the world for Christ.[2]

SANGUINE
(The Influencer)

Influencer
Initiator
Inspirer
Interest in people
Interacter

Motivated by:

People, approval, and recognition

Goal:

To persuade others by creating an environment that motivates and assembles people to influence others

Strengths and Weaknesses:

STRENGTHS	WEAKNESSES
• Optimistic	• Overselling
• Enthusiastic	• Manipulative
• Personable	• Self-centered
• Charismatic	• Emotional
• Confident	• Overconfident
• Communicative	• Compulsive talker
• Persuasive	• Poor listener
• Gregarious	• Superficial
• Sense of humor	• Exaggerative
• Compassionate	• Angers easily
• Life of the party	• Disorganized
• Memory for stories	• Bored with detail
• Innocent	• Naive
• Good on stage	• Insecure

Best Environment:

- Freedom from control and detail
- Opportunity to influence others
- Friendly

Biggest Fear:

Rejection

Reaction to Stress:

Attacks verbally

Suggestions for Personal Growth:

- Listen more.
- Discipline yourself to follow through.
- Control your time and emotions.
- Condense your conversation.
- Follow through on friendships.
- Say no to extra responsibilities.
- Be sensitive to others.
- Don't come on so strong.

To discover if you are a sanguine personality, take the survey at the end of the chapter. If this is your primary personality type, then rejoice that God will use you to have such a persuasive influence on people, and make it a goal to increase your effectiveness by asking God to help you discipline yourself to overcome your weaknesses.

PHLEGMATIC
(The Relater)

Sympathetic
Stable
Steady
Sensitive
Security conscious
Supportive

Motivated by:

Relationships and appreciation

Goal:

To support the present environment by encouraging positive relationships and specializing in specific tasks and consistent roles

Strengths and Weaknesses:

STRENGTHS	WEAKNESSES
• Loyal	• Avoids conflict
• Supportive	• Unenthusiastic
• Agreeable	• Conforming
• Relational	• Possessive
• Easy-going, relaxed	• Complacent
• Balanced	• Indecisive
• Consistent	• Limited goals
• Sympathetic and kind	• Fearful and worried
• Diplomatic	• Unspoken expectations
• Dependable	• Undisciplined
• Reluctant leader	• Misses opportunities
• Sincere	• Lenient
• Quiet listener	• Spectator
• Contented	• Lethargic

Best Environment:
- Specialized opportunities with parameters
- Working with a team consistently
- Supportive appreciation

Biggest Fear:
Loss of security

Reaction to Stress:
Passively yields

Suggestions for Personal Growth:

- Acknowledge self-worth.
- Take initiative to participate.
- Set goals.
- Don't procrastinate.
- Make key decisions daily.
- Broaden range of friendships.

To discover if you have a phlegmatic personality, take the survey at the end of the chapter. If this is your primary personality type, discover how God can use you to build positive, long-term relationships that will support your present environment. Ask God to help you take initiative to overcome your weaknesses.

MELANCHOLY
(The Thinker)

Contemplator
Conscientious
Competent
Creative
Controlled
Correct/analytical
Calculating
Compliant

Motivated by:

Excellence, accuracy, protection, and security

Goal:

To accurately create a product that meets the highest standards of excellence

Strengths and Weaknesses:

STRENGTHS	WEAKNESSES
• Precise	• Too careful
• Orderly	• Picky
• Thorough	• Too detailed
• Cautious	• Too cautious
• Analytical	• Analysis paralysis
• Systematic	• Obsessive/compulsive
• Accurate	• Indecisive
• Conscientious	• Detached
• Adaptable	• Sensitive
• Creative	• Finicky
• Quiet	• Withdrawn
• Self-sacrificing	• Martyr complex
• Faithful	• Too involved
• Perfectionist	• Judgmental
• Thinker	• Depressed
• Humble	• Self-negating

Best Environment:

- Supportive and predictable
- Clearly defined standards of excellence
- Operating with precision and accuracy

Biggest Fear:

Criticism, change

Reaction to Stress:

Withdraws

Suggestions for Personal Growth:

- Loosen the grip on perfection.
- Don't take it personally.
- Risk verbalizing your feelings.
- Think positively.
- Control emotional highs and lows.
- Respect others with their imperfections.
- Accept change.

Take the survey at the end of the chapter to find out if you have a melancholy personality. If this is your primary personality type, then analyze how God will use you to create artistry and excellence in the body of Christ. Design a plan to increase your effectiveness, and ask God to help you overcome your weaknesses.

The Focal Point

Positives and negatives. Strengths and weaknesses. Probably you will discover some things about your personality that you like and some you don't like. (Unless, of course, you are Choleric!) You will make some fascinating discoveries about your teenagers too. How you relate to each other given your unique and possibly different personalities is critical during the teenage years. In the appendix you will find some helpful insights into how you as a parent relate to your kids generally with your own personality (Parental Personality Tendencies). And you will discover how your specific personality relates to the specific personality of your child (Parenting with Personality). On page 172 in the appendix, you'll also find biblical personality profiles to help you better understand your own.

Because of our imperfections we will never have total balance in our personalities. But Jesus, the Perfect Man, was the perfect balance of all four of these personality types. Because of that, and because He lives in us to accomplish His purposes for us, He can adjust our personalities to become like His. When we release His Spirit in us, He works in our unique personality to help us live to reflect His glory. When that process is going on, we get voted Best Personality every day of the week!

Get Ready

1. Take the **Discovering My Personality Survey** on page 54 and then score it yourself. Follow the instructions.
2. Talk to someone about what you learned about yourself from the survey.
3. After you and your teenager take the test, review both of your personality types. In light of your unique personalities, make some notes on Parental Personality Tendencies and Parenting with Personality to determine how you relate and/or conflict with your teenager. Keep your notes with you as a reminder.
4. Pray for God to show you how to relate to your teenager better in light of your new understanding of both of your personalities.

To pursue this further, write or fax to Reach Out Ministries to purchase the DISC Personality Profile. The cost for each test is fifteen dollars.

Reach Out Ministries
3961 Holcomb Bridge Road
Suite #201
Norcross, GA 30092
Phone: (770) 441-2247
Fax: (770) 449-7544
Email: 72002.1704@compuserve.com

HELPING MY TEENAGER GET READY

1. Pray for your teenager to have deep insight into his or her personality.
2. Have your teenager work through chapter 5 and then take the **DISCOVERING YOUR PERSONALITY SURVEY** together.
3. Talk over the results by answering the questions in Funtalk.

FUNTALK

1. Let's talk about what we discovered about ourselves and each other. Let's answer these questions:

    - Am I like the test indicated?
    - What is my personality type? What major characteristics do I identify with?
    - How do I see myself differently now than before I took the test?
    - What do I like about myself? (Strengths)
    - What does God need to change? (Weaknesses)

    Refer to the tests and the pages in the chapter about the various personalities.
2. Let's pray for a deeper understanding of ourselves and each other.

Parents' Group Discussion

1. Give each person a sheet of poster-sized paper and a marker. Have all of them list the following:
    - their personality type
    - three characteristics of their personality type with which they most identify
    - the three major strengths of their personality
    - the three major weaknesses of their personality
2. Discuss the sheets. Divide into smaller groups if time is a factor.
3. On the back of that same sheet write down your teenager's personality type, three characteristics, three strengths, and three weaknesses.
4. Referring to Parental Personality Tendencies and Parenting with Personality, how do you identify with and/or conflict with your teenager in personality.
5. Pray for the ability to relate to your teenager with more understanding now that you both comprehend each other's personalities better.

DISCOVERING MY PERSONALITY TEST

Each of us is a combination of the four basic personality types. No one particular personality is any better or any worse than the others. They are all different. Therefore, there are no right or wrong answers.

In each of the twenty-four lines, you have a choice of four words or phrases. Choose the word or phrase that best describes you when you are with your family and your friends.

Follow these two steps to complete the test.

1. Circle the one word or phrase on each of the twenty-four lines that best describes you. Circle only one per line. Choose the word or phrase that describes how you really are, not what others expect of you, or how you wish you were.
2. Determine your score by locating the word or phrase on line 1 that you circled and matching it to the column letter at the top. Find line 1 of the Scoring Sheet and locate the matching letter. Circle the column letter. It will not necessarily be the same column as the test.

For example, on line 1 if you circled "daring, pioneering," it is under column B. Go to line 1 on the Scoring Sheet and circle the "B." You will note that it is now under column 1.

Once you have transferred all answers from the test to the Scoring Sheet, add up the total number of circles in each column and place that number on the line at the bottom of that column. These four numbers should total twenty-four.

The column you score highest in is your dominant personality type.

Column 1—Choleric (The Doer)
Column 2—Sanguine (The Influencer)
Column 3—Phlegmatic (The Relater)
Column 4—Melancholy (The Thinker)

Now that you know your personality type review the characteristics of your personality on pages 43–50.[3]

DISCOVERING YOUR PERSONALITY SURVEY

Directions: Circle ONE phrase in each row that you feel describes you best.

	A	B	C	D
1.	gentle, kind	daring, pioneering	humble, mild-mannered	persuasive
2.	stubborn	careful	likable	considerate
3.	patient	sociable	bold	analytical
4.	decisive	listens	easy going	free-spirited
5.	precise, accurate	funny	slow to get angry	forceful
6.	inspiring	self-reliant	tactful with words	thinks of others
7.	perfectionist	team-player	will not give up	wants to have fun
8.	motivator	brave	unsure	mediator
9.	friendly	exact	even-tempered	competitive
10.	thinks things through	shows feelings	insistent	balanced
11.	decision-maker	sacrificing	mild-mannered	talkative
12.	easily pleased	respectful	full of life	daring
13.	enthusiastic	aggressive	tends to worry	easy going
14.	cautious	understanding	takes charge	gets agreement
15.	expresses emotion	detailed	agreeable	loves challenges
16.	confident	animated	one thing at a time	analytical
17.	self-disciplined	suspicious	lively	predictable
18.	energetic	kind	adventurous	chooses carefully
19.	quiet	positive	willing to please	tries new things
20.	argumentative	examines closely	easily led	does not worry
21.	demanding	trusting	contented	critical of self
22.	repetitious	indecisive	has many friends	controlling
23.	supportive, helpful	fun to be with	decides carefully	outspoken
24.	gets along easily	questioning	popular	wants change

SCORING SHEET

1.	B	D	A	C
2.	A	C	D	B
3.	C	B	A	D
4.	A	D	C	B
5.	D	B	C	A
6.	B	A	D	C
7.	C	D	B	A
8.	B	A	D	C
9.	D	A	C	B
10.	C	B	D	A
11.	A	D	C	B
12.	D	C	A	B
13.	B	A	D	C
14.	C	D	B	A
15.	D	A	C	B
16.	A	B	C	D
17.	B	C	D	A
18.	C	A	B	D
19.	D	B	C	A
20.	A	D	C	B
21.	A	B	C	D
22.	D	C	B	A
23.	D	B	A	C
24.	D	C	A	B
	______	______	______	______

My personality type is ______________________.

6 Pull Out the Credit Card

What are your teenager's spiritual gifts, and how can he or she use them?

"Hey, Dad, can I have some money?"

Has your teenager ever said that before? What was your response?

- "No!"
- "Not in your lifetime."
- "Not again."
- "Do you think money grows on trees?"
- "This is it! That's all! No more!"

Why do you give a negative response? Money doesn't grow on trees. Resources are limited.

It would blow your teenager away if sometime you said, "Sure, how much do you need? Spend all you want. Here's my credit card. Have a great time!"

GOD HAS ISSUED US A CREDIT CARD with unlimited resources. We can use the card whenever we need it. Through what He gives us we have enough for other people too. And unlike our credit cards, we never have to pay it off. Here's how it works.

God's grace in us
gives spiritual gifts to us
to accomplish God's work through us.

Some people are afraid of spiritual gifts. They think, "I'm not getting into this because once you discuss spiritual gifts, then handling snakes can't be far behind." Yet without spiritual gifts we lack power to overcome the forces of darkness. With them we bring the power of Christ into any situation. Spiritual gifts are vital to discovering our destiny.

With spiritual gifts we can bring the power of Christ into any situation.

Many Christians experience lack of fulfillment because they do not know their spiritual gifts and how to use them. But when we know our spiritual gifts, then we will be able to parent better and to serve Christ better. When our kids discover their gifts, they will be more motivated and spiritually alive. Parents either burn out or miss out in doing God's work because they do not grasp the tremendous motivation and energy that spiritual gifts provide. Yet with these gifts in operation we have the sensitivity and ability to minister to our children, and they in turn are sensitized and enabled to minister to us. As a family we have what it takes to make a difference with our friends, in our neighborhood, and at school. That's why the apostle Paul told us, "Now about spiritual gifts, brothers, I do not want you to be ignorant" (1 Cor. 12:1).

God's Grace in Us

In Romans 12:6 the apostle Paul laid the groundwork that leads us into the discovery of our unique gifts. We have different gifts according to the grace given us.

Charis

We came into a relationship with Christ by the grace of God (Eph. 2:8–9). At that point we received The Gift—Jesus Christ Himself. The Greek word for grace is *charis*. Grace is . . .

God's
Riches
At
Christ's
Expense

Charisma

When we entered into a relationship with Jesus, He placed His Holy Spirit within us. The Greek word for that is *charisma*. We have the gift of the Holy Spirit continually pouring into us and filling us up, like a spring bubbling inside us, giving us the resources we need to live the Christian life.

Charismata

Part of what we receive are spiritual gifts. The Greek word for gifts is *charismata* ("gracelets"), little graces or spiritual gifts. All of our little gifts come from the big gift of grace.

Char

When we use those gifts, they bring great joy. The Greek word for joy is *char*. Not only do we experience joy ourselves when we use our gifts, but also we bring joy to others.

God Gives Spiritual Gifts to Us

Since spiritual gifts come from the Holy Spirit, certainly we do not want to misuse them any more than we would want to misuse a valuable credit card. Avoid these errors:

1. "My spiritual gifts are my natural talents and abilities." A beautiful singing voice is not a spiritual gift; it is a natural talent. We don't measure our effectiveness for Christ by our talents and abilities. What we have to offer God *naturally* isn't enough. Spiritual gifts allow us *supernaturally* to tap into the resources of God.
2. "Spiritual gifts are not for today." The overwhelming needs of people today require us to conclude that only by releasing God's power through spiritual gifts can we make a difference in people's lives.
3. "Only mature Christians can use spiritual gifts." The Bible never equates spiritual maturity with spiritual gifts.
4. "I will choose my spiritual gift." We don't choose our spiritual gifts. God chooses them and then gives them to us. The emphasis is not on us, but on Him.

Avoiding these errors frees us to use our spiritual gifts more wisely.

On the positive side we will use our gifts better when we understand who they are for. The credit card has your name on it.

- Every Christian has spiritual gifts. When you received Christ, He brought with Him the gifts of the Spirit. As Ron Dunn has said, "When the Holy Spirit enters into the believer, He doesn't come empty-handed." The apostle Peter made that very clear when he instructed us: "As each one has received a *special* gift, employ it in serving one another" (1 Pet. 4:10, NASB).

- Each one of us has received the very best gifts for us. God wants us to have the very best gifts possible so He picked them out personally and then delivered them individually to us. The apostle Paul hammered that point home when he said, "All these are the work of one and the same Spirit, and he gives them to each one, just as he determines" (1 Cor. 12:11).

To Accomplish His Work through Us

Like strong muscles give strength to our physical bodies, spiritual gifts put to use make the body of Christ strong. Spiritual gifts are the "muscle" to the body of Christ. When I broke my wrist and had my arm in a cast for six weeks, I learned how quickly muscles atrophy when they are not in use. Conversely, lifting weights three times a week builds my muscles. That is why the apostle Paul challenged the Romans regarding spiritual gifts, "let him use it" (Rom. 12:6).

When spiritual gifts are in use, then the body of Christ functions properly.

- The body is built up. Gifts are not for selfish advantage. Paul said, "All of these must be done for the strengthening of the church" (1 Cor. 14:26). Everyone benefits when we use our gifts.
- The body experiences unity. A body has many different parts. Every part is needed for the body to function properly. A plastic surgeon who designs prosthetic body parts said in *People* magazine, "The body is made to be symmetrical. If one part is missing the body does not function in balance. All of the parts are needed." Then he showed how putting an ear on a little girl restored her balance. After explaining spiritual gifts Paul wrote about the body: "The body is a unit, though it is made up of many parts; and though all its parts are many, they form one body. So it is with Christ . . . those parts of the body that seem to be weaker are indispensible" (1 Cor. 12:12, 22).
- The people in the body care for each other's needs. When spiritual gifts function in an environment of love, people have the ability to meet each other's needs. Paul went on to say that not only should "its parts . . . have equal concern for each other," but also, "If one part suffers, every part suffers with it; if one part is honored, every part rejoices with it" (1 Cor. 12:25–26).

We can split the different spiritual gifts into three categories according to 1 Corinthians 12:4–6:

1. "different kinds of gifts"—grace gifts
2. "different kinds of service"—service gifts
3. "different kinds of working"—working gifts*

Each of these three groups of gifts serves a different purpose. Let's take a closer look so we can know the gifts God has for us and our teenagers, and how we can use them to pursue our destiny.

Grace Gifts

These gifts come directly from God's grace and give us *motivation* for ministry. They give us the energy to build God's kingdom. We find these gifts in Romans 12:6–8.

1. *Prophesying.* A prophet brings messages from God to people, usually revealing ungodly motives and attitudes in others.
2. *Serving.* A servant demonstrates love by meeting practical needs.
3. *Teaching.* A teacher researches and validates truth, then helps others understand this truth.
4. *Encouraging.* An encourager stimulates the faith of others.
5. *Giving.* A giver entrusts resources to others to carry out the ministry.
6. *Leading.* A leader coordinates the activities of others to achieve common goals.
7. *Showing mercy.* A merciful person identifies with and comforts those in distress.

* All gifts are an extension of God's grace. Yet here and in the other passages about gifts the apostle Paul places the gifts in different categories. In 1 Corinthians 12:4–6 he uses three words for gifts: (1) *Charismaton,* which means "grace." In Romans 12:6 he uses the same word for gifts, referring to spiritual gifts of grace. He gives a list of those gifts. (2) *Diakonian,* which means "service." In Ephesians 4:12 he uses the same word after listing the gifts. (3) *Energematon,* which means "work" and from which we get the word *energy.* This word indicates power that is in operation. This energy or power manifests itself in spiritual gifts. Paul then gives a list of the gifts that manifest themselves in 1 Corinthians 12:7–11. This is a helpful way of looking at the gifts but by no means the only way of approaching it.

While you are eating lunch at a fast-food restaurant someone slips. The tray of burgers, fries, and drinks flies through the air and crashes to the floor. Food covers a ten-foot radius. All around people stare and snicker.

How would you respond as a

1. *Prophet?* "That's what happens when you're not careful."
2. *Servant?* "Let me help you clean it up."
3. *Teacher?* "You fell because the floor was slick and the tray was too heavy on one side."
4. *Encourager?* "Next time walk more slowly and carry your tray with both hands. It won't happen again."
5. *Giver?* "I'll buy you another lunch."
6. *Leader?* "Tom, let's clean up. You get the mop, and Sue, you get the tray."
7. *Merciful person?* "Don't feel too bad. It could happen to the best of us."

Your response to this situation will give you an idea of what your "grace gift" might be.

SERVICE GIFTS

These *ministries* give us opportunities to take action and serve others (1 Pet. 4:10). They fit against a backdrop of love that cares deeply about other people. Before the apostle Peter launched into an explanation of service gifts, he said, "Above all, love each other deeply, because love covers over a multitude of sins" (1 Pet. 4:8). Because we love, we serve with our gifts, giving them freely to minister to others.

Let's summarize these gifts as found in Ephesians 4:11; 1 Corinthians 12:27–31; and 1 Peter 4:10.

1. *Apostles.* Apostles are those sent forth with authority to advance the kingdom of God and build up the church.
2. *Prophets.* Prophets speak for God.
3. *Evangelists.* Evangelists announce the good news of Jesus publicly and privately and equip Christians to witness to their faith.
4. *Pastors.* Pastors shepherd the flock with care and guidance.
5. *Teachers.* Teachers search the Word of God and explain it to others.

6. *Miracle workers.* Miracle workers do signs and wonders to build up the church and to demonstrate the power of God to an unbelieving world.
7. *Healers.* Healers bring physical, emotional, and spiritual healing to people.
8. *Helpers.* Helpers serve by meeting needs, particularly those of the poor and sick.
9. *Administrators.* Administrators give leadership to the church.
10. *Tongues-speakers.* Those who speak in tongues communicate with God in a special prayer language.

The grace/motivation gifts are put into practice in the context of these service/ministry gifts. Once you discover your grace gift, you find a place to put it into practice through one of the service gifts.

Working Gifts

This set of gifts offers *manifestations* or outward expressions as a result of the Holy Spirit working in our lives. In 1 Corinthians 12:7–11, the word "manifestation" means God gives to us these different gifts, giving one here and one there at various times and in various situations. As opposed to grace gifts, which we have permanently, these gifts come and go. We never *possess* them, we *express* them. Why? God wants to give us just what we need to meet the situation of the moment.

1. *Wisdom.* Wisdom is seeing from God's point of view.
2. *Knowledge.* Knowledge is gaining insight into a specific situation.
3. *Faith.* Faith is visualizing what God wants to do.
4. *Healing.* Healing means giving spiritual, emotional, or physical health.
5. *Miraculous powers.* Miraculous powers means allowing God to demonstrate His power supernaturally.
6. *Prophecy.* Prophecy is expressing the message of God to others.
7. *Discernment.* Discernment is perceiving hidden attitudes.
8. *Tongues.* Tongues means communicating with God in a special prayer language.
9. *Interpretation of tongues.* Interpretation of tongues means translating spiritual truth after someone speaks in tongues.

These gifts are given "for the common good." When these gifts operate, then everyone in the body profits as a result.

From each person's *grace gift* (motivation) can come a variety of different *service gifts* (ministry). When someone exercises his or her service gift, then any number of *working gifts* (manifestations) can be expressed.

DISCOVERING YOUR SPIRITUAL GIFTS

At this point you must ask: "So, how do I discover my spiritual gifts?" And at the same time be aware that you can help your teenagers discover theirs. Follow these practical steps.

1. *Believe.* Trust that God has given you spiritual gifts. Jesus lives in you, and God has promised His gifts to you. Open your heart and mind to what the Lord has for you. Don't reject your gifts because of your past experience, fear, lack of knowledge, or preconceived ideas. Accept them according to "the measure of faith God has given you" (Rom. 12:3).
2. *Receive.* If Christ lives in you, you already have spiritual gifts. "You do not have, because you do not ask God" (James 4:2). Ask God to show you what your gifts are by praying a prayer like this: "Lord Jesus, Giver of all good and perfect gifts, I desire to receive the gifts You have for me. Please show me what they are and how to use them."
3. *Study.* Make a thorough study of spiritual gifts. Reread: Romans 12:3–8; Ephesians 4:11–13; 1 Corinthians 12:27–31; 1 Peter 4:10; 1 Corinthians 12:7–11; and 1 Corinthians 14.
4. *Confirm.* Your desires and experiences and the advice of others all fit into the discovery process. Use these practical hints to confirm your gifts.

    - Take the spiritual gifts test. What did it say about your gifts?
    - Examine your personal desires. What do you enjoy doing most? This gives you a clue to what your gifts are, but it is not necessarily conclusive.
    - Experiment with your gifts. If you are not sure what your gifts are, then try the ones you think might be yours. When you try one, if it is yours, then you will enjoy the challenge of using it.
    - Talk to people you respect. Go over this material with your pastor or a respected friend. Get their input.

5. *Respond.* With gifts come opportunities to use them. As you use your gifts, you will discover and confirm them. How does God want you to use your gifts to minister to others?

   - Use your gifts to energize the body of Christ. The Great Commandment is to love God with all of our hearts, and to love our neighbors as ourselves (Matt. 22:36–38). By using our gifts we energize others with love and build up the body of Christ.
   - Use your gifts to evangelize the lost. The Great Commission tells us to "go and make disciples of all nations" (Matt. 28:18–20). When we exercise our spiritual gifts around non-Christians, then God will use us to bring people to Christ.[1]

Once you know your gifts and your teenager knows his or her gifts, then you will not only be personally enriched, but also you will share an incredible spiritual understanding of each other that will allow you to appreciate each other more and to minister together from your own uniqueness. You will both enjoy it more than an unlimited credit card!

Get Ready

1. Take the **Spiritual Gifts Survey** at the end of the chapter and then talk to others about your gifts.
2. Determine the best place for you to experiment with your spiritual gifts this week. Try using your motivation gift and record how that worked out.

____

____

____

____

Helping My Teenager Get Ready

1. Pray for your teenager to discover and use his or her spiritual gifts.
2. After your teenager works through the lesson on his or her own, plan to take the **Spiritual Gifts Survey** together and then discuss it. Use the Funtalk questions.

3. Help your teenager figure out a place and opportunity where he or she can use the gifts. After both of you experiment with this, discuss how it went and where you go from here.

FUNTALK

1. Let's take the **SPIRITUAL GIFTS SURVEY** together and see what we discover.
2. After taking the survey, say to your teenager, "Tell me what you think your motivation gift is and I'll tell you mine."
3. Do you think the survey was correct? (Go back over the survey questions that had to do with your gifts. Discuss your answers. If your teenager is unsure, go over the test again.)
4. Let's go back to the illustration of the dropped tray in the restaurant. Does the survey confirm how you would respond?
5. Let's figure out how we can use our gift in a practical way to honor and serve Christ. Where can we try out our gifts? (Make plans to try your gifts.)
6. Let's pray that God will use our spiritual gifts to the maximum potential.

PARENTS' GROUP DISCUSSION

1. Write your spiritual gift on a card. Shuffle the cards, pass them out, and see if you can guess who has what gift.
2. Then give the cards back to the original owners. Ask participants individually to explain why they think they have that particular gift in light of the restaurant tray illustration on page 62.
3. See if any are unsure about their gifts. If so, work on it as a group to help them come to a positive conclusion. Go back to the chapter material if necessary.
4. If you have done this with your teenager, talk about his or her gifts and how he or she wants to put them into practice.
5. Consider doing a group project together on Saturday morning. Perhaps you could feed people at a homeless shelter. Use the project as an opportunity to experiment with and use your gifts.
6. Pray for yourselves and your teenagers by name that you will be able to maximize the use of your gifts for the glory of Christ.

SPIRITUAL GIFTS SURVEY

This survey[2] is designed to help you discover your basic motivational gift. It is not a foolproof method; however, it will provide a guideline. For some who take the survey, it will become obvious what their spiritual gift is. For others it will help them to narrow down to two or three the most likely possibilities.

Instructions for Taking the Survey

1. Please answer every question. Do not leave any questions blank.
2. There are no right or wrong answers to any of the questions. Answer the questions as they apply to you.
3. Mark the answers with

   + (usually characterizes me)
   o (sometimes characterizes me)
   – (hardly ever characterizes me)

Scoring Instructions

1. Complete the survey, answering every question.
2. On the page entitled "Tally Sheet for Spiritual Gift Survey," add the numbers for each category to discover the total. The one you have the most of is your primary motivation gift.

Identifying Your Spiritual Gifts

1. I easily recall specific likes and dislikes of people.
2. I enjoy making wise purchases and investments.
3. When another person has problems, I like to see what needs to be done and offer steps of action.
4. I am free to feel happy or sad when I am with an individual or group.
5. I like to discover and meet practical needs, especially manual projects.
6. I have a desire to give money to valuable projects or ministries.
7. I avoid giving people information that lacks practical application to their lives.

8. I am attracted to and understand people who are in distress.
9. I have the desire to meet needs as quickly as possible.
10. I give my money hoping to get others to give.
11. I have the ability to see how people's problems can help them reach new levels of maturity.
12. I have a desire to remove hurts and bring healing to others.
13. I don't get tired when I meet others' needs.
14. I see financial needs that others might overlook.
15. I have more concern for people's mental distress than for their physical distress.
16. I am willing to use my personal funds to avoid delaying a project.
17. I enjoy meeting needs without someone putting pressure on me to do it.
18. I like to discover insights from people's human experiences that can be backed up in Scripture.
19. I avoid confrontation unless I see how it will benefit another person.
20. I like to see a job completed, even if I have to give extra effort to finish it.
21. I enjoy it when my money is an answer to specific prayer.
22. I like it when people are eager to follow potential steps of action.
23. I am sensitive to words and actions that hurt other people.
24. I consult with another person to confirm the amount of a gift I want to give.
25. I don't like it when someone teaches me something that does not have practical steps of action.
26. I have the ability to sense sincere motives in other people.
27. I am involved in a variety of activities and find it difficult to say no.
28. I have a concern that my money goes to quality individuals and ministries.
29. I enjoy talking to people when it results in new insights for them.
30. I enjoy short-range goals but get frustrated with long-range goals.

31. I like to feel a part of the people or work to whom I give my money.
32. I feel close to those who are sensitive to the needs and feelings of others.
33. I experience frustration when time limits are attached to jobs.
34. I do not feel close to those who are insincere or insensitive.
35. I like to verbally express what God has shown me.
36. I have the ability to see the big picture and to set long-range goals.
37. I believe that the gift of teaching is the foundation for all other gifts.
38. I can discern the character and motives of others.
39. I like to organize the things for which I am responsible.
40. I like words to be accurate when I talk and write.
41. I am able to identify, define, and hate evil.
42. I like to complete tasks as quickly as possible.
43. I like to challenge the knowledge of those who teach me.
44. I am willing to confess my sins if it encourages others to confess theirs.
45. I like to know the resources available to me to complete a task.
46. I like to do research in order to prove the truth of the Bible.
47. I like to depend on the Bible as my highest authority.
48. I know what can or cannot be delegated.
49. I like to see people's behavior change to match their convictions.
50. I like to move on to a new challenge.
51. I like to systematically study and teach the Bible.
52. I like to speak to others directly to persuade them to action.
53. I tend to assume leadership if no structured leader exists.
54. I don't like illustrations unless they come from the Bible.
55. I have a deep concern for God's reputation.
56. I will endure negative reactions from workers in order to accomplish the task.
57. I get turned off by illustrations from the Bible that are out of context.

58. I hurt over the sins of others.
59. I get excited when a plan comes together, and I enjoy seeing the finished product.
60. I enjoy doing detailed research of the Bible more than I enjoy presenting it.
61. I like to help other people see their personal weaknesses.
62. I like people to pay attention when I speak to them.
63. I like to test myself against principles in the Bible.

TALLY SHEET FOR SPIRITUAL GIFT SURVEY

Instructions: Add the numbers under each category.

2 points for +
1 point for o
0 points for –

Serving

1____ 5____ 9____ 13____ 16____ 20____ 27____ 30____ 33____

Total ____________

Giving

2____ 6____ 10____ 14____ 17____ 21____ 24____ 28____ 31____

Total ____________

Exhortation

3____ 7____ 11____ 18____ 22____ 25____ 29____ 35____ 62____

Total ____________

Mercy

4____ 8____ 12____ 15____ 19____ 23____ 26____ 32____ 34____

Total ____________

Prophecy

38____ 41____ 44____ 47____ 49____ 52____ 55____ 58____ 61____

Total ____________

Leadership

36____ 39____ 42____ 45____ 48____ 50____ 53____ 56____ 59____

Total ____________

Teaching

37____ 40____ 43____ 46____ 51____ 54____ 57____ 60____ 63____

Total ____________

7 Go for the Best

What are your teenager's abilities and experiences, and how can he or she maximize them?

Comic books! I love 'em! When I was growing up, I read all kinds. I collected them. All of the comics had one thing in common. The back page had the Charles Atlas ad. Always the same, the headline read: "ARE YOU TIRED OF BEING A 6 FOOT, 90 POUND WEAKLING?" "Yep," I said. I read on. The first frame was a skinny guy and a beautiful girl at the beach together. In the second frame a muscular bully kicked sand in the skinny guy's face. In the third frame "Mr. Muscle" strolled off with the girl. The fourth frame showed the skinny guy kicking a chair and yelling, "I'm tired of being a 6 foot, 90 pound weakling!" He filled out the Charles Atlas coupon in the fifth frame. In the sixth frame he received his Charles Atlas kit and began working out. Six weeks later, in the seventh frame, our frail friend had transformed into Mr. Olympia. In the final frame he got the girl back.

Every comic book I opened, I read the Charles Atlas ad. Why? I identified with the skinny kid. I hoped my body would change. It never happened!

EVERYTHING AROUND US "SUCKERS" us and our teenagers into the world's view of what we are supposed to look like, smell like, and dress like, but God does not look at our potential the way the world does.

When we look at our teenager's potential from a strictly human perspective, usually we fall into a ditch on either side of the road. We can have too high a view of our child's potential. We think Junior is the greatest, the most fantastic, the best. If other parents scatter when we come around, it could be from the nausea they experience when we espouse our child's incredible talent. Conversely, we can communicate to our teenagers: "You're no good." "You will never amount to anything." "Can't you do anything right?" Often, even when we don't say it, that negative message gets communicated to our children. Hopefully, as we explore the issues of ability and experience, instead of going into the ditch on either side of the road, we can keep ourselves moving down the highway with God's perspective.

> Do not think of yourself more highly than you ought to think, but rather think of yourself with sober judgment, in accordance with the measure of faith God has given you. (Rom. 12:3)

WAY BEYOND US

Do you ever dream about your teenager's future? His or her potential? Certainly! But rarely do we dream big enough. Usually we dream in light of limited abilities and confined experiences. God wants to work through their abilities and experiences to move beyond them.

When Jesus asked the disciples, "Who do you say I am?" Peter, the disciple, responded with limited potential written all over him. When we look at Peter's abilities and experiences, we wonder how the Lord could ever use him. (I wonder what his mom thought?)

- He had "foot in mouth disease." At the holy moment of the transfiguration with Jesus in deep conversation with Moses and Elijah, Peter broke the mood with his inappropriate obnoxious comment: "Master, this is a great moment! What would you think if I built three memorials here on the mountain . . ." (Matt. 17:2, THE MESSAGE).
- He appeared to have an IQ just above plant life. (Well, not quite that bad!) For three years Jesus had talked of peace and love. When the soldiers came to arrest Jesus, Peter forgot it all. He pulled his sword and "taking a swing at the Chief Priest's servant, cut off his ear" (Matt. 26:51, THE MESSAGE).
- He was rude and crude. When Jesus made it clear to His disciples that He had to go to Jerusalem to die, Peter had a few choice words for Him: "Impossible, Master! That can never be!" Jesus told him to get out of the way, that he was on Satan's side" (Matt. 16:22, THE MESSAGE).
- He exhibited little self-discipline. Jesus had told Peter, along with the other disciples, to watch and pray. Instead they all fell asleep—not just once, but three times (Matt. 26:38–45).

- He was filled with fear. Peter protested that if everyone else abandoned Jesus he would not. Within a few hours a teenage girl intimidated him. He denied Jesus for the third time (Matt. 26:69–75).

In spite of Peter's inabilities and lack of experience, he answered Jesus' question "Who do you say I am?" correctly. In one of the greatest statements ever uttered, Peter proclaimed, "You are the Christ, the Son of the living God" (Matt. 16:16).

God took the limited abilities and experiences of this common fisherman, converted them, and then established His church on Peter, the rock. Like Peter, God wants to take our limited abilities and experiences, and those of our teenagers, convert them, and then use us to do things that are way beyond us—things that will cause us to live to reflect His glory.

Converted to the Cause

Where Peter may have had limited talents, the apostle Paul was totally different. He had terrific talent.

- Paul had business skills. As a rabbi, according to Jewish practice, Paul had to have a trade. He could take no money for preaching, so he made his living as a tent-maker, a skilled craftsman (Acts 18:3).
- He was a genius. He had mega-intelligence. Paul "reasoned in the synagogue" (Acts 18:4). He could do that because he was so well educated. Acts 22:3 indicates that Paul studied under Gamaliel, the greatest teacher of his day.
- He was sophisticated. We know that Paul possessed Roman citizenship, indicating that he was a man of culture (Acts 22:28).

But he had a dark side. Zealous in all he did, Paul had it out for the young church. From Acts 7:59–8:3 we see that he stood by giving approval when Stephen was stoned. Paul then took it upon himself to go from house to house, dragging believers out of their homes and putting them in prison.

God tapped all of these positive abilities and negative experiences when He met this man on the Damascus Road and converted his skill, intelligence, culture, and misplaced zeal toward one cause—taking the gospel to the Gentiles. The apostle Paul lived to reflect His glory.

As He did with Peter and Paul, God wants to convert our abilities and experiences and those of our teenagers and use them for His cause.

What is the principle? People have talent—some less, some more. People have experiences that are part of their lives—some bad, some good. In it all God converts our abilities and experiences, then uses them to accomplish His purpose.

With that principle in mind, how can we practically maximize our abilities and experiences for God's purpose?

1. *Understand that everyone has unique abilities and experiences.*

One of the most common excuses people give for not getting involved is, "I just don't have anything to offer."

That seems to be what one person thought in the parable of the talents (Luke 19:11–27). Have you ever wondered what the one-talent guy was thinking when he buried his talent?

- Not smart enough?
- Not esteemed enough?
- Not trained enough?
- Not good enough?

All of those servants, including "Mr. One Talent," had some significant things going for them. They had

- something to invest.
- the responsibility to invest it.
- time to make the investment.
- the promise of a return on the investment.
- the promise of multiplied rewards.

What was true of those servants is true for us. But like the servant who didn't invest his talent, often we fall prey to common myths about what God has given us to invest.

Myth 1: I have very few skills.
Myth 2: I can't do much because I was not born with skills.
Myth 3: Valuable skills are learned primarily in the classroom.
Myth 4: If I have skills, I will know I have them.
Myth 5: Skills I use at work or school cannot be used elsewhere.[1]

The truth is that each of us have certain talents. National studies show that the average person possesses five hundred to seven hundred skills. Some may be sharpened in the classroom, others by experience. Through experience we begin to identify our many skills. We may use them in our work, but we can also use them in ministry. Our unique abilities and experiences open the way for God to use us uniquely.

2. *Quit comparing ourselves to others.* When we crank up the comparison approach, we get our nose bloodied badly.

THE WORLD SAYS	WE SAY
"Look glamorous."	"I look average."
"Be wealthy."	"I'm struggling to pay for my sneakers."
"Act macho."	"I'm a wimp."
"Be intelligent."	"I feel dumb."
"Athletes are cool."	"I'm spastic."
"Rock stars are heroes."	"I can hardly play the radio."

In the spiritual realm it's even worse. We know we should read the Bible, pray, and witness. When we go to church and hang around Bobby Bible Study, Priscilla Prayer, and Wally Witness, we get intimidated quickly.

If we accept the world's view of success, then we will always feel inferior. We will never measure up.

However, the apostle Paul lifted us out of that pit with a fresh perspective in 2 Corinthians 10:12. "We do not dare to classify or compare ourselves with some who commend themselves. When they measure themselves by themselves and compare themselves with themselves, they are not wise."

Practically, we can quit comparing ourselves and our teenagers to others by agreeing with God daily:

- God created my unique self.
- He put me together in my mother's womb.
- His works are wonderful.
- When He made me, He did not make a mistake. He made me so unique that, like the snowflake, there is no one else like me (Ps. 139:13–14).

At a prestigious southern college I learned this. I decided to major in history. I made a 74 on my first history test. Redoubling my effort, I made a 47 on the second test. So much for history! My roommate became a Fulbright scholar. A fraternity brother earned a Rhodes scholarship. By comparison I felt dumb and dumber. I didn't measure up. In a vicious cycle I beat up on myself by comparing myself to these very intelligent people. But then I made the revolutionary discovery that I have "the mind of Christ" (1 Cor. 2:16). In time I quit comparing myself to other people, and God began to use my unique mind to communicate His thoughts to others.

3. *Maximize strengths and minimize weaknesses.* Write your name in the box.

Now write your name with your opposite hand.

Quite a difference! When we can't write with our preferred hand, then it makes us feel uncomfortable. Writing takes extra time and effort, and we do a lousy job of it. But when we write with the hand that has "ability and experience," we not only feel comfortable at it, but also we do it quickly and excellently. We never think, "I need to work on writing with my other hand." Why? We build on our strength, not fret over our weakness.[2]

When I ask people, "What are your five greatest strengths?" they struggle to answer me. When I say, "Tell me your five greatest weaknesses," they do it in a heartbeat. We tend to focus more on our weaknesses than on our strengths. How can we turn that around and build on our strengths?

- *Realize that God did not design us to do everything.* A friend once said, "Barry, you're the kind of person who likes to eat the whole pizza in one bite." He correctly observed that I want to do it all. From him I learned to focus, only doing the few things God has given me to do.

- *Recognize that we will never have some abilities, no matter how hard we try.* I could practice sixteen hours a day and never become an accomplished musician. I just don't have it. The psalmist gave us God's perspective: "I praise you because I am fearfully and wonderfully made; your works are wonderful" (Ps. 139:14). God made us "wonderfully," even without some abilities because He can use us best that way.

God is not finished with us yet!

- *Turn difficult experiences into opportunities.* Victimized by our background or scarred by sinful choices, different experiences have created weaknesses in us that have to be overcome. Simon Peter had those weaknesses too. He swore allegiance to Jesus loudly, then denied Jesus because of his fatal flaw of wanting to please everyone. But the Holy Spirit turned that flaw—his fear of rejection—into fearlessness. Peter boldly led three thousand people to Christ in one day.

As president of the student body in high school, I gave a speech in assembly every week. Fearful and insecure, I wrote out the speeches word for word and read them. Once Jesus took control of my life, He turned my fear of speaking into something I enjoy so much I do it for a living.

- *Concentrate on inward strength, not outward ability.* In our society, ability, beauty, and talent are gods. But the true God cares more about character than coolness. When God sent Samuel to find a king for Israel, immediately Samuel saw Jesse's handsome son, Eliab, and thought he had found the king. Then Samuel learned that God had a better idea. "But the Lord said to Samuel, 'Do not consider his appearance or his height, for I have rejected him. The Lord does not look at the things man looks at. Man looks at the outward appearance, but the Lord looks at the heart'" (1 Sam. 16:7).

My wife, Carol, and I have tried to capture that with our kids since they were very young. I wish I had a dollar for every time I have told my girls, "To be pretty on the outside, you have to be pretty on the inside." That beauty comes as we learn to obey Christ.

- *Cooperate with God to finish the job.* God is not finished with us yet. He will continue to sharpen our strengths and minimize our weaknesses. According to Romans 8:28–29, He is committed to shaping us to become more and more like Jesus Christ.

4. *Give our best to serve others for God's glory.* How do you think God views our abilities and experiences?

   If our teenagers are

- athletically gifted, does He want them to be a star?
- physically attractive, does He want them to become a model, actress, or homecoming queen?
- musically talented, does He want them to sing publicly?
- intelligent, does He want them to make all A's or big bucks?

Many people lose touch with God's plan right here. In fact, many become bitter because they asked God to make them or their children a success, and in their view He didn't do it. Why not? God is not into producing superstars, but servants. He operates on a higher principle than our personal success. His rule of thumb: "Whether you eat or drink or whatever you do, do it all for the glory of God" (1 Cor. 10:31).

The bottom line is,

God wants us
to use our abilities and experiences
to serve others
for His glory.

When we put God ahead of our own success, then we free ourselves to excel in every area of life for the glory of God. The same will be true with our teenagers. Jesus modeled that when He washed His disciples' feet. Then He said, "Now that I, your Lord and Teacher, have washed your feet, you also should wash one another's feet" (John 13:14). Jesus had the ability and experience to do anything, but He chose to serve others for God's glory. He challenges us to model that same approach to success with our teenagers. Then we, and they, will live to reflect His glory!

Get Ready

1. Take the **Abilities Survey** on page 83.
2. Take the **Experiences Survey** on page 85.
3. In light of what you have learned, what one change will you make in the use of your abilities and experiences?

Helping My Teenager Get Ready

1. Pray for your teenager to have God's perspective on his or her abilities and experiences.
2. Take the **Abilities Survey** and the **Experiences Survey** with your teenager.
3. Share the survey results and how you can apply them using the discussion questions in Funtalk.

Funtalk

1. What did you discover about your abilities and experiences that caused you to see yourself differently than before? Be specific. (Review the chapter if necessary.)
2. Let's look at the **Abilities Survey** and talk about what we think we do best.
3. Let's look at the **Experiences Survey** and decide what we consider the five most important experiences of our lives and why.
4. In light of what we have learned, what one change do each of us need to make in order to use our abilities and experiences for the glory of God?
5. Let's pray that God will show us how to better use our abilities and experiences for His glory.

Parents' Discussion Group

1. Using markers and old magazines, design a collage that shows your five most significant abilities and your five most significant experiences. Tell why they are important.
2. What is one important change you need to make in order to better utilize your own abilities and experiences for the glory of God?

3. If you have done this session with your teenager, then design a collage on the back of yours that shows your teenager's most important abilities and experiences and tell why he or she felt they were important.
4. Pray for each other and for your teenagers by name that they will use their abilities and experiences for God's glory.

ABILITIES SURVEY

Make a list of your five most fulfilling accomplishments.

1. ____

2. ____

3. ____

4. ____

5. ____

Now go back and circle the verbs that show the actions you performed in each achievement.

Check the five most significant abilities you have:

- Entertain: perform, act, dance, speak, model, sing
- Recruit: enlist, motivate people to get involved
- Interview: discover what others are really like
- Research: read, gather information, collect data
- Draw: conceptualize, picture, paint, photograph, cartoon, caricature
- Graph: lay out, design, create visual displays or banners
- Evaluate: analyze data and draw conclusions
- Plan: strategize, design, and organize programs and events
- Manage: supervise people and coordinate the details to accomplish a task
- Counsel: listen, encourage, guide with sensitivity
- Teach: explain, demonstrate, tutor, train
- Write: produce articles, letters, books
- Edit: rewrite, proofread
- Promote: advertise events and activities
- Repair: fix, restore, maintain
- Feed: create meals for large or small groups
- Recall: remember names, faces, or information
- Mechanically operate: use equipment, tools, or machinery
- Resource: search out inexpensive approaches
- Account: work with numbers, data, or money
- Classify: systematize and file books, data, records, material

- Relate: deal with people with care and courtesy
- Welcome: develop rapport, convey warmth, make people feel comfortable
- Compose: write music, lyrics
- Landscape: garden, work with plants, beautify the outdoors
- Decorate: beautify a setting[3]

Combining the lists of your five most fulfilling accomplishments and your five most significant abilities, write down your top five:

1. ______________________________
2. ______________________________
3. ______________________________
4. ______________________________
5. ______________________________

EXPERIENCES SURVEY

Write your brief autobiography by recording your three most significant experiences at each age level. Consider the following types of experiences as you think about it:

- spiritual experiences (most meaningful decisions/times with God)
- family experiences (memories—positive and/or negative)
- painful experiences (problems, hurts, trials)
- educational experiences (favorite subjects, best teacher, where you learned the most)
- ministry experiences (opportunities to serve, witness)

Ages 1–12

1. ______________________________
2. ______________________________
3. ______________________________

Ages 13–18

1. ______________________________
2. ______________________________
3. ______________________________

Ages 19–22

1. ______________________________
2. ______________________________
3. ______________________________

Ages 23 to present

1. ______________________________
2. ______________________________
3. ______________________________

What do you consider the five most significant experiences in your life? Why?

1. ______________________________
2. ______________________________
3. ______________________________
4. ______________________________
5. ______________________________

Write down a final "Top 10" list of your abilities and experiences:

1. ______________________________
2. ______________________________
3. ______________________________
4. ______________________________
5. ______________________________
6. ______________________________
7. ______________________________
8. ______________________________
9. ______________________________
10. ______________________________

Where is the primary place you can use these abilities and experiences for God's glory?[4]

____

____

____

____

8 Give It All

What motivates your teenager, and how does he or she give 100 percent?

2:27 P.M. I bolted out of class and ran to the gym for basketball practice. I arrived first and left last. From 2:45 until 5:00 every school day I practiced with the team. I wanted to hit more shots, make more free throws, win more sprints than anyone else on the team. With limited talent, my scrawny six-foot body was dwarfed in a big man's game. But I worked hard. I stayed after practice from 5:00 until 6:30 to work out on my own. In the summer I practiced eight hours every day and played in games three nights a week. I loved every minute of it. Nothing had a more beautiful sound than the ball bouncing on the floor and then swishing through the net. Often I wondered, What motivates me? Am I motivated for the right reasons?

HIGH AND HEALTHY MOTIVATION AMONG the younger generation is in short supply these days. The prevailing philosophy of kids today is "I don't care." "It doesn't matter." "No big deal." I have surveyed thousands of youth leaders about the biggest struggle they face in their youth ministries. Almost 100 percent of the time they answer "apathy." They say, "We can motivate students for fun and entertainment, but they split when it comes to spiritual issues." What do youth leaders say is their second biggest struggle? "Parents. They are more spiritually apathetic than the students."

As parents, motivation must become a major focus of our attention with our kids. Without it they will go nowhere in any of these other areas. We must take a critical look at our own motives and then help our kids with theirs.

Only *wholehearted motivation* propels people toward their destiny. The words of Paul, the apostle, move us in the right direction. "Whatever you do, work at it with all your heart, as working for the Lord, not for men" (Col. 3:23).

This is what we are shooting for with our kids. Whether they pursue photography, business, homemaking, or friendships, or hundreds of other interests, we need to help them invest every ounce of their energy into it for God's glory.

The other side of the coin of lack of motivation is wrong motivation. Many parents get into the Little League Syndrome. They ruin something positive by using the wrong kind of motivation. That can have a devastatingly negative effect on our children.

Sharon's desire for achievement (a positive) combined with her fear of failure (a negative), almost ruined her. A highly skilled, successful All-State athlete, she broke down in sobs as she told me her story. To her it seemed like no matter how well she did, it was never quite good enough for her dad. She told me, "I can't ever please him. I can't take it anymore. I quit. I don't care."

So then, how do we, as parents, strike the right balance in motivating our teenagers?

TOTAL MOTIVATION

When we pursue God's destiny for us, we can approach it only one way—with all of our hearts. That is total motivation!

Frequently I tell my wife, Carol, "Honey, I love you with all of my heart." But what if I told her, "Carol, I love you, but there are three other women I want to be with. I can only live with you . . . let's see . . . 25 percent of the time." Or what if I said, "Carol, I love you 95 percent of the time, but I want to see this other woman 5 percent of the time." Would you think I loved my wife? The only way to love her is with all of my heart.

As parents, we move away from total motivation when we focus on our kids' external behavior.

My daughter Katie played on her first basketball team at age eleven. The first game our girls got clobbered because all five of them hovered around the ball. After the game I told Katie I would teach her to get the ball out of that clump of girls and drive to the basket. Every day we worked on driving to the basket. I drilled her: "Get the ball and drive to the basket." The next Saturday the same gals in the same blue uniforms did the same thing they had done the week before—they hovered around the ball. I knew Katie would grab that ball and drive to the basket. But she didn't. I told Carol, "She is not driving to the basket." I called out to Katie, "Drive to the basket!" Still no response. I yelled it louder, "Drive to the basket!" It wasn't happening, so I yelled really loud as she was coming up the court, "Drive to the basket, Katie." She stopped in the middle of the court, put her hands on her hips, and yelled back, "Dad, I'm trying to drive to the basket." How embarrassing! External motivation at its finest failed!

Total motivation does not come from external behavior but from internal desire.

After a weekend of fever, our son, Scott, then fifteen, wasn't getting better. We took him to the hospital Monday morning. What started as a bad day got worse. By the end of the day the doctors had a tube in his lungs, fearful that he might not make it through the night. I called some men in our church to pray. As we gathered around his bed, the Lord gave us two prayers. One, that God's healing hand would touch him during the night in such a way that the doctors would know that it was God who did it, not medicine. Two, that the Lord would speak to Scott in his unconscious state about his life.

The next morning the nurse said, "Barry, it's like Scott's lung was black and now it is white." The doctors met later to discover what had caused such a radical change. When I went in the room, Scott was very animated, even though he could not talk because of the tube in his lungs. He wrote on a pad:

> The other day on the news it said that the number of deaths related to the flu and pneumonia had reached epidemic proportions. When I found out about double pneumonia, it threw me for a loop. Lately my Christian walk has not been growing but at a standstill. Last night the Lord changed my view of Him, the world, and myself. He's put His vibrant Spirit wholeheartedly back into me. I woke up today praising the Lord just to be alive and exalting Him. Every time the nurses woke me up to do testing during the night, they said I had a great big smile on my face. I woke up singing, "This is the day the Lord has made." [Then he wrote in large letters]
>
> "PRAISE THE LORD!"

That experience internally motivated Scott to the degree that through high school he lived for Christ, and at Duke University he took on his fraternity as his mission. Now in medical school as a result of this experience, Scott and his wife are pursuing medical missions.

God creates total motivation internally when we open ourselves up to Him and say, "I want You with all my heart." As parents, we are shooting for that intrinsic motivation for ourselves and for our kids. However, three "heartbreakers" desire to steal that total motivation.

HEARTBREAKER 1: WRONG MOTIVES

Many people are totally motivated, but often with the wrong motives. Jesus called these wrong motives "evil" after He gave us a list of them. "For from within, out of men's hearts, come evil thoughts, sexual immorality, theft, murder, adultery, greed, malice, deceit, lewdness, envy, slander, arrogance and folly. All these evils come from inside and make a man 'unclean'" (Mark 7:21–23).

We tend to think of the negative characteristics on this list as "big time" sin. But all of these big sins begin with little motives. If we feed them, they grow until they suck godly motives out of us and pump evil desires into us. Then they control us.

God desires to turn evil motives into pure ones. He wants to clean up our unclean motives. That begins when we honestly confess our wrong motives and ask God to "cleanse us from all unrighteousness" (1 John 1:9, NASB).

Once we repent and confess, that becomes an attitude, a lifestyle, that continues to reveal any wrong motives that crop up in our lives. As we ask to "be filled with the Holy Spirit" (Eph. 5:18), our wrong motives will turn into right ones.

HEARTBREAKER 2: MIXED MOTIVES

Some people fall into the trap of half-heartedness. Their motives aren't necessarily wrong, but they are mixed. They dabble at this and that, doing good things but not God's best thing. So they meander through life not sure why they do what they do.

Mixed motives have flooded the church in America. George Gallup's polls show that 81 percent of Americans say they are born again, but only 42 percent know that Jesus delivered the Sermon on the Mount and only 46 percent could name the four Gospels. And 60 percent of the church's young people are sexually active. What's the problem?

The trap is wanting the best of both worlds. People want enough of God to have the good things that come with Jesus, but they desire what the world offers too. They think they can straddle the fence. They think they can drink and party on Saturday night and worship on Sunday. It doesn't work. Like the wishbone of a chicken, they feel the pull. A person can only stand that pressure for so long.

The apostle James called these people "double-minded." He described them as "unstable in all [their] ways" (James 1:8, NASB). That kind of person is like "a wave of the sea, blown and tossed by the wind" (James 1:6). In case that imagery does not grab our attention, James also said, "What causes fights and quarrels among you? Don't they come from your desires that battle within you? You want something but don't get it. You kill and covet, but you cannot have what you want. . . . You do not have, because you do not ask God. When you ask, you do not receive, because you ask with *wrong motives,* that you may spend what you get on your pleasures" (James 4:1–3, author's italics).

But James didn't stop with the negative. He turned the problem of double-mindedness into an opportunity for wholeheartedness. Look at what God does to get people out of the half-heartedness trap in James 4:6–8.

First, He releases His grace (v. 6). Grace defined is God's supernatural ability in us through the cross and resurrection. Grace acts as the springboard that gets us out of the mixed motives trap and lands us in the circle of pure motives. We step on the springboard when we take these simple steps.

1. Submit ourselves to God (v. 7). We let God take control of our motives. We release our negative, selfish desires, as well as the good things—like our children.
2. "Resist the devil" (v. 7). Satan stands ready like "a roaring lion" to "devour" our positive motives (1 Pet. 5:8). We need to pray against the devil's influence in our lives that would keep us from pure motives.
3. "Come near to God" (v. 8). Daily we need to refocus our motives. We can do that when we spend time with God every day. Set aside at least thirty minutes a day to "come near to God."

In time God will purify our hearts through these steps. Instead of giving in to the tug toward half-heartedness, we will have a totally intense desire to please God.

HEARTBREAKER 3: WEAK MOTIVES

Fatigue, frustration, discouragement, burnout, exhaustion, stress, despair—a wave of circumstances can wash over even our pure motives and wipe us out.

When we become fainthearted we may sound like this: "I have the 'spiritual blahs.' My Christian life has lost its focus. I am no longer motivated to live for Christ. I could not care less. What's wrong with me?"

The apostle Paul described the fainthearted as one who can potentially "lose heart" (2 Cor. 4:16). Because of our battle with the world, the pressures of everyday living, our own overcommitment, and satanic oppression, we may find ourselves on the edge of exhaustion.

When we identify the specifics that gnaw at our wholeheartedness, then we can design solutions that cause us to say with Paul, "We do not lose heart" (2 Cor. 4:16). For example, we may just be tired. The solution: get a good night's sleep. It's amazing what a good night's sleep will do to change our perspective!

The most powerful weapon on earth is the human soul on fire. (Ferdinand Fock)[1]

On another level our outward circumstances may not change. They may continue to wear us down. But "inwardly we are being renewed day by day" (2 Cor. 4:16). If we have the right perspective, these "light and momentary troubles" push us toward Christ, building eternity in our hearts.

> That happened to Katie. A serious car wreck and a torn knee ligament within the span of a year overwhelmed her at first, but in the end they strengthened her motivation. These troubles helped her to "fix [her] eyes not on what is seen, but on what is unseen" (2 Cor. 4:18). Instead of "taking her out," these difficulties drew her in to a more intimate relationship with Christ. The change in her has been significantly evident.

Going through difficult challenges can either take us out or draw us in. As we and our teenagers confront difficulties and allow them to draw us in, then we purify our motives and that leads us into total motivation.

The Heart Builder: Total Motivation

A receiver on a football team runs full speed downfield, jumps in the air with his arms extended while two 250-pound line-backers converge on his ribs. All of this is to catch a cheap piece of polished pigskin with Wilson written on it.

People give 100 percent for much less noble purposes than God's purpose. We need that same 100 percent approach toward Jesus Christ. He desires us to "love the Lord your God, with all of your heart and with all your soul and with all your mind and with all your strength" (Mark 12:30). God wants 100 percent of our

- emotions,
- personality,
- intellect, and
- bodies

to go toward loving Him. That's wholeheartedness.

C. T. Studd, the most famous cricket player in nineteenth-century England, gave up his bright future in sports after Cambridge University. He had decided to go to China as a missionary with six other young men. They were known as the Cambridge Seven. When a group of students asked why, Studd replied, "If Jesus Christ be God and died for me, then no sacrifice can be too great for me to make for Him." Then he asked them: "Have you surrendered everything to Jesus Christ? Because if Jesus is not Lord of all, then He is not Lord at all."

How can we, and our teenagers, possess that kind of 100 percent, wholehearted spiritual motivation? When we embrace these simple but profound steps as our daily attitude and lifestyle, then we will insure that our hearts wholly belong to the Lord. Our teenagers will possess that same wholehearted motivation when they embrace these steps as well.

1. *Repent.* Let God's searchlight shine continually into every corner of your life to find anything that is not totally under His control.
2. *Seek.* If we seek Him, we will find Him. The more we find Him, the more we will want to seek Him. Pray this prayer daily: "Lord, today I am seeking to find You in every person and situation."

3. *Obey.* Obedience means taking action that goes against the grain of our personal desires. Make "Yes, Sir" your answer to the Lord no matter what the question is.
4. *Serve.* Daily look for ways to give time, energy, and money for the cause of Christ.
5. *Rejoice.* Surrender doesn't mean somber. Instead of taking away the fun in life, He will give you more fun.

More than anything else we do with them, our wholehearted motivation will influence our teenagers to have a passion for the Lord themselves. They will catch it from us and they, in turn, will become highly motivated to live to reflect His glory.

GET READY

1. To identify your motives and motivations, take the **MOTIVES AND MOTIVATION TEST** on page 96.
2. In light of what you discovered, make sure that you write out your plan at the end of the test. Take one action today to turn a negative motivation into a positive one.

HELPING MY TEENAGER GET READY

1. Pray for your teenager's motivation. Ask God to speak to him or her, reveal negative motives, and turn them into positive ones.
2. Take the **MOTIVES AND MOTIVATION TEST** at the same time your teenager takes it.
3. After you complete the test, discuss the results using the Funtalk questions.

FUNTALK

1. Let's talk about what we learned about ourselves from taking the test. I'll share my biggest struggle first, then you can share yours. (Do this with all three of the struggles you listed at the end of the test.)
2. Now let's go back and talk about our plans to move toward total motivation. Let me tell you my first one. (Do this with all three of the plans you wrote.)
3. Can we agree to hold each other accountable for one action we will take on this during the week? Which action?

4. Pray for each other's struggles and plans. Pray for total motivation for both of you.

You may discover some struggles with your teenager that you did not anticipate. Do not hesitate to get help. Offer to go together to see your youth leader, your pastor, or a counselor.

Parents' Discussion Group

1. On a scale of 1–10 (1 lowest, 10 highest) what is your general level of motivation?
2. Why? To answer that, let's go to the three struggles at the end of the Motives and Motivations Test.
3. Using the plans you designed at the end of the test, tell what actions you need to take to raise your motivation level.
4. Discuss this question: "How do I reach a healthy balance between accepting my teenager where he or she is (unconditional love) and getting him or her to reach a certain level of performance and achievement?" (Record your insights on a marker board so you stay focused.)
5. Minister to any parents who are having a particular struggle with motivating their kids. Pray for them as a group. Meet with them afterwards. Get them in touch with a counselor if necessary.
6. Pray for each teenager by name. Pray that Mark 12:30 will become each teenager's heart's desire.

MOTIVES AND MOTIVATION TEST

To decide which of these issues hinders pure motives or stifles your motivation, use a scale of 0–5 to indicate the degree of your struggle with it. (0 is no struggle; 5 is total struggle). Make a list of your "Top Three" at the end of each section. Follow the instructions at the end of the test.

WRONG MOTIVES

	0	1	2	3	4	5
Evil thoughts						
Sexual immorality (messing with sex)						
Theft (stealing, cheating)						
Murder (hateful thoughts or actions intended to hurt someone)						
Adultery (sex outside of marriage)						
Greed (materialism)						
Malice (hatred)						
Deceit (lying, cheating)						
Lewdness (obscene language or actions)						
Envy (jealousy)						
Slander (gossip)						
Arrogance (pride)						
Folly (party animal)						

TOP THREE:

1.

2. ______________________________

3. ______________________________

____

MIXED MOTIVES

In this section make a list of two under each question, and then proceed with the instructions.

	0	1	2	3	4	5

1. What do you worry about most?
   1. ____________________
   2. ____________________
2. On what do you spend most of your money?
   1. ____________________
   2. ____________________
3. In what do you place your security?
   1. ____________________
   2. ____________________
4. What makes you feel important?
   1. ____________________
   2. ____________________
5. What do you daydream about?
   1. ____________________
   2. ____________________

TOP THREE:

1. ____
2. ____
3. ____

WEAK MOTIVES

Which of these pressures cause you to lose motivation?

	0	1	2	3	4	5
Negative attitudes						
Wrong priorities						
Burnout						
No time with God						
Negative talk						
Disappointment						
Guilt						
Overcommitment						
Poor eating habits						
Broken relationship						
No time with family						
Fatigue						
No exercise						
Work stress						
Fear						

TOP THREE:

1. ______________________________
2. ______________________________
3. ______________________________

Total Motivation

Choose the three you struggle with the most out of the total list and write them in the blanks below.

1. ______________________________

2. ______________________________

3. ______________________________

Write out your specific plan to turn negative motivation into positive motivation.

____

____

____

____

____

Walk through the steps on page 93-94 to write your plan.

1. ______________________________

My plan: ______________________________

____

2. ______________________________

My plan: ______________________________

____

3. ______________________________

My plan: ______________________________

____

If you marked any categories in the 4–5 range, talk to a Christian friend, your pastor, or a counselor to help you get these under God's control.

How Am I Going to Get There?

9 Aim at the Target

What is your teenager's life purpose, and how can he or she discover it?

He went deerhunting at every opportunity. His wife had never gone. She insisted that he take her. He told her, "It will be cold, dark, and the briers will scratch you." She persisted. They went. He was right. The morning was cold and dark, and the briers did scratch her. When they got to a clearing, he showed her how to shoot the gun. Then he put her on the deer stand and went off through the woods. About a hundred yards away, he heard bang, bang, bang! He hustled back through the brush, got back to the edge of the clearing, and saw his wife pointing her gun at a man. He was standing with his hands in the air. She was yelling, "That's my deer. That's my deer. You get away from my deer." The man yelled, "OK, lady, OK, just let me get the saddle and the bridle off."

THIS WOMAN DID NOT KNOW WHAT to aim for! As we zero in on our purpose in life, we want to make certain that we aim at the right target.

TAKING AIM

An ad in *Newsweek* stated: "Last year Americans traveled 350 billion miles and never found what they were looking for."

Without purpose, we are like the turnpike close to my home in West Virginia. It's the turnpike that "starts nowhere and ends nowhere." Without purpose we're traveling, but going nowhere.

As a parent and youth leader, I agree with Albert Camus, the philosopher: "Here is what frightens me. To see the sense of this life dissipated. To see our reason for existence disappear. That is what is intolerable. Man cannot live without meaning."[1]

I estimate that 90 percent of the thousands of Christian young people I talk to each year are like that. Actually it was out of that discovery and for the sake of my own children that I started this *Life Happens: Get Your Teenager Ready* study. Think about it. Where can teenagers discover their purpose? No secular high school or college curriculum teaches values much less helps young people with their purpose. Rarely do churches or Christian schools address the subject specifically. So how do our children discover it? They don't unless they either "happen on it" or learn it from us as parents. Out of that vacuum we have the great privilege of helping our kids discover their purpose!

THE TARGET

Our purpose is our target. If we miss it, we miss the entire reason for our existence.

How can we describe "purpose"? Our purpose

- drives us
- keeps us awake at night
- wakes us up in the morning
- causes us to jump out of bed with enthusiasm
- gets us excited
- expresses our hopes and dreams
- is our North Star
- is worth dying for

Even though most people don't know what they are aiming for, that does not have to be true of you. You can locate the target, take aim, and fire!

Soon after I began to follow Christ, someone sent me this message on a card.

Only one life, twill soon be past;
Only what's done for Christ will last.

As a young Christian it helped me target my purpose.

The apostle Paul knew the target. In Philippians 3:8 he exclaimed with great enthusiasm the value of knowing Christ: "What is more, I consider everything a loss compared to the surpassing greatness of knowing Christ Jesus my Lord, for whose sake I have lost all things. I consider them rubbish, that I may gain Christ."

With intense focus he went on to express the purpose of his life. "I want to know Christ and the power of his resurrection and the fellowship of sharing in his sufferings, becoming like him in his death" (Phil. 3:10).

Let's start at the outer edge of the target and work our way to the bull's-eye. Once we know our general purpose, we can more easily discover our unique, specific purpose.

To Know Him

To what lengths would you go to meet a superstar? Knowing Jesus is a million times more valuable than meeting Michael Jordan. Why?

Blaise Pascal, one of the greatest scientists and philosophers of all time, wrote, "Apart from Jesus Christ, we know not what our life is, nor our death, nor God, nor ourselves."[2]

That puts a high premium on knowing Christ. But what does it mean?

"To know" is more than

- learning a few simple facts about Jesus
- reading the Bible occasionally
- having some vague religious experience
- joining a church

"To know" means an intimate, personal relationship. Closeness, communication, warmth, and love are part of knowing Christ. That is why when Jesus called His disciples, they considered knowing Him of such value that they left everything and followed Him (Matt. 4:20).

> As Leonardo da Vinci painted "The Last Supper," a crowd watched over his shoulder. He was working on the fruit on the table. When he saw that the crowd had their eyes glued on the fruit, angrily he stroked across the fruit, obliterating it. Pointing to the face of Christ, he said, "Don't look down there, look up here."

Aim at knowing Jesus. He is the target.

To Make Him Known

> Asked how he could make such beautiful figures out of a plain block of marble, a famous sculptor replied: "I picture a tiger in my mind, then I hammer and chisel on that block of marble until everything is gone but tiger."

That's what the apostle Paul had in mind when he said we are to become "like him" (Phil. 3:10).

How does "becoming like him" make Him known to others? More than becoming an evangelist or missionary we make Jesus known by reflecting Him in every thought, attitude, word, and action.

Only through the power of the resurrection (God's hammer) and the fellowship of His suffering (God's chisel), can He work in us and on us until we are transformed to become like Him.

Without purpose we're traveling, but going nowhere.

The power of His resurrection. Because Christ lives in us, we have the same power living in us now that raised Jesus from the dead. Through that power we can change to become like Him.

To get some idea of our power to change, compare the resurrection power to a nuclear bomb. One nuclear bomb can destroy the world 267 times. Yet all the nuclear bombs in the world do not begin to demonstrate the power that it took to raise Jesus from the dead. That unique power can help us live in a way that reflects Jesus Christ and makes Him known to others. Through the power of the resurrection we can know God's purpose for us and accomplish it.

The fellowship of His sufferings. People love power. But suffering never draws a large crowd. Yet sharing in Christ's sufferings comes as part of the "purpose package." "Why doesn't God just take away my problems so I can be happy?" Because suffering transforms us into the image of Christ. When life is a bed of roses, we tend to lose the intensity of wanting to know Christ. But when pressure pursues us, we turn to Him. That is why the apostle Paul called it a gift "granted to you" (Phil. 1:29).

> Everything I touched when I was growing up turned into success. Then in my first year of college everything I touched seemed to fail. My grandmother, who was my closest friend, died just before I left for college. No matter how hard I tried, I didn't do well in academics or athletics. On Homecoming Weekend my date stood me up. All of my friends came in drunk. I woke up that Saturday morning and stared out the window with a deep emptiness. For the first time in my life these questions flooded my mind: "Who am I?" "What am I doing here?" "Where am I going?" Even though it took several months to discover the answers, it was out of that sense of futility, my first suffering, that I launched out on the journey to find my life purpose.

Cancer, the death of a loved one, or rejection in a relationship chip self off of us and create a God-shape in us. That is what Romans 8:28 really means. Often trivialized or dismissed with cynicism, the truth is that "all things" actually do "work together for good for those who love God, who are called according to his purpose" (NRSV). God allows "all things" in our lives to press us on toward our purpose that we may be "conformed to the likeness of his Son" (Rom. 8:29).

God wants to use His power and our difficulties and problems to make us and our teenagers more and more like Him! The more we become like Him the more we fulfill our purpose.

The Bull's-eye

Now that we have hit the target—to know Him and make Him known—let's take aim at the bull's-eye, our specific purpose.

Years ago Dianna Ross of "The Supremes" fame phrased the question well about our purpose.

Do you know where you're going to?

To express the question more graphically, when people gather around your casket to pay their last respects, what do you want them to say about you?

> "Your life can be represented by a straight line that has as its origin your birth and an arrow on the opposite end indicating the unknown time of your death. None of us know how long we will have in this life, but let's say you have lived close to twenty years and you have approximately fifty years left. Here is the question: When you come to the end of those fifty years, and you have nothing but death to look forward to and nothing but memories to look back upon, what will you need to see for you to conclude, 'My life was a success?'"[3]

A fun evening with the family is not sitting around thinking about when we are going to die. However, to discover our life purpose, we have to begin there. "All planning begins at the end," someone said. When we call a travel agent to plan a trip, what is the first question they ask? "What is your final destination?" Thinking about our final destination will help us determine our purpose now.

What is your unique, specific life purpose? What is your teenager's?

For an example I have included mine.

My purpose is

To *seek* Jesus Christ and *serve* Him
by *equipping* youth leaders, students, and parents
for strategic ministry.

A longer, more inclusive version reads like this.

My purpose is

To *seek* Jesus Christ and *serve* Him
by *equipping* youth leaders, students, and parents
for strategic ministry through:

- *becoming a leader worth following*
- *communicating the message of Christ clearly*
- *encouraging the coming awakening*
- *involving my family with me*

in order to glorify Jesus Christ and
fulfill the *Great Commission.*

The bullets will become the basis for the goals you will set to accomplish your purpose later on in the book. I worked on my purpose statement for several months before I completed it the first time. I have revised it on several occasions since then.

The more we become like Jesus the more we fulfill our purpose.

For both ourselves and our teenagers, Mack Douglas summarizes the significance and value of targeting our life purpose: "What is the difference in one man and another? Here's a man who is dynamically, enthusiastically, vibrantly alive. Everything he does is charged with power. Here's another who droops, drags and meanders through mere existence. The difference is purpose. There is amazing power in purpose."[4]

Get Ready

1. Ask yourself the Five Questions in **The Purpose Discovery Exercise** on pages 111–12, praying for the Lord to reveal His specific, unique purpose to you.
2. Follow the Five Instructions in the exercise in writing your purpose statement. Make sure you go through the three stages of writing it to avoid getting yourself bogged down. Keep working on it until you come up with your final purpose statement.
3. Share your purpose statement with at least one other person. Get feedback on whether or not it hits the bull's-eye of your uniqueness.

Remember: Don't try to do all of this in one sitting. Work on it some each day until you are comfortable with it. This takes time and effort. Take the time and put in the effort. It will help you the rest of your life.

Helping My Teenager Get Ready

1. Ask the Lord to give your teenager discipline to work on his or her life purpose. Pray that God will make His purpose very clear.
2. Work through **The Purpose Discovery Exercise** with your teenager. Set aside thirty minutes several nights to work on it together. Don't hurry the process.
3. Talk about what each of you is discovering in the process. Use the Funtalk questions.

FUNTALK

Break these down into thirty minute sessions each night.

- *First night:* What do you want your epitaph to say? Here is what I wrote.
- *Second night:* How would you summarize what you wrote in the Five Questions?
- *Third night:* Let's go through the Five Instructions and write our purpose statement together (Follow the instructions on p. 111.) Finish this on the fourth night. You will need the time.)
- *Fourth night:* Let's finish the Five Instructions and finalize our life purposes.
- *Fifth night:* Go together to a T-shirt shop and get your life purpose printed on a T-shirt. If you can't do a T-shirt, get the purpose statement printed or laminated.

PARENTS' DISCUSSION GROUP

1. If possible, have a white T-shirt and markers for everyone. Write your life purpose on the shirt and then share it with the group. (If a T-shirt is not available, use pieces of a sheet.)
2. Why do you think writing down one sentence is such hard work? Why is it so valuable? (Give them an opportunity to vent their frustrations in working on this.)
3. In groups of two, walk through the answers you wrote for the Five Questions. Give your answers in quick, summary form.
4. Talk about how the nightly sessions went with your teenager. (If they have their teenagers' life purpose with them, let them share it.)
5. Pray for your teenager by name asking God to make his or her purpose Christ-centered, clear, and a guide for life.

THE PURPOSE DISCOVERY EXERCISE

Look at some specific guidelines that will help you discover your purpose.

Five Questions

Ask yourself these specific, penetrating questions. Jot down notes as you think through each one. Pray, asking God to reveal His specific purpose to you.

1. Why do I exist?

2. What do I want my epitaph to say? When I die, what do I want my friends and family to say about me?

3. How am I totally unique?

4. What do I feel deeply burdened about?

5. What does God want me to do?

Five Instructions

Using the Five Questions as background, follow these instructions to write your purpose.

1. Pray: "Lord show me Your purpose for me."
2. Make your purpose statement broad.
3. Realize that this statement should span your entire life.
4. Understand that you do not have to express end results or measurable goals. That will come later.

5. Write your purpose statement using the following three steps.

   - *Write your statement any way you want.* Make it as long as you like. Let this flow. Don't get uptight thinking that if you write something, you will never be able to change it.
   - *Write three key words.* From what you wrote above identify the three action verbs that express what you want to do with your life.
   - *Write the final statement.* Using the three key words above express your purpose as one, brief, clear, easy-to-understand sentence. Write it down on the next page. Remember: It should fit on a T-shirt!

   Once you write your purpose statement to your satisfaction, type it. Keep it with you all the time. Memorize it. Verbalize it to others. Carry it in your wallet. Place it in the front of your notebook.

MY LIFE PURPOSE

10 Know Which End is Up

What are your teenager's values, and how can he or she define them?

Rod and I were to fly from Oklahoma City to Sante Fe on a commercial flight. As we stood in the hall discussing our plans, a fellow we knew, overhearing our conversation, offered to fly us in his small, private plane. Never having flown in a small plane, both of us looked at each other with that "no way" look. But that is not what came out. "I will if you will," I blurted. "Well, I will if you will," he challenged. We went.

At the airport the wind was blowing so hard that when our pilot unlatched the plane it whipped around like a wild dog on a leash. When we loaded the luggage, the tires kept getting lower and lower! We had to manually turn the propellers to get it started. I wanted out!

Instead we got in, Rod in the back and me in the front. We sput . . . sput . . . sputtered down the taxiway. About halfway down the runway the thought hit me, This is nothing but a go-cart with wings. Before I could process that, a clump of trees was staring us in the face. I thought, We're dead. At the last moment the pilot pulled back the stick, and we cleared the trees by inches.

Higher and higher we went, until it seemed like we could see all of Oklahoma. Now more fascinated than fearful, I asked lots of questions. Rod was quiet in the back. Then the pilot asked me, "Do you want to fly the plane?" Before I could respond, he flipped the steering wheel in front of me. Vrooooom! The plane veered to the right. Vrooooom! The plane veered to the left. By the time I got control, Rod was "white-knuckling" in the back.

Then moments later a large cloud appeared. I asked about going around it. Under it? Would you believe over it? "No—through it." I knew it was only a cloud. Nothing more than condensed water, I recalled from eighth grade science. My conscious mind was saying, "Cloud," but my subconscious mind kept shouting, "Wall!" I pictured myself becoming a grease spot on impact. Sure enough, we eased into the cloud. I couldn't see *anything. We were at it again. Vroooom! Vrooom! After the third or fourth "vrooooom," I took a quick glance to the back. White as a sheet, Rob grabbed for the vomit bag.*

Grabbing the controls as the plane lurched, the pilot muttered, "St. Clair, you don't know which end is up." The rest of the trip he flew by instruments.

FLYING BY THE INSTRUMENTS

THAT PLANE RIDE WAS LIKE LIFE. As we go places we have never been and do things we have never done, our lives can easily veer out of control. We mutter, "I don't know which end is up." But if we do know which end is up and navigate by the instrument panel of our values, not only will we avoid crashing, we can move toward God's destiny for us.

Therein lies the problem both for us and for our teenagers. We live in a post-Christian era that has created a values vacuum. Whose values? What values? Anarchy reigns on the campus. Violence, drugs, and teenage sex issues scream at us daily in the media. No one seems to know how to stop us from sliding down the slippery slope. In our own individual, personal way we as parents must put our finger in the dike and do our part to stem the tide. We can do that with the principles and plan presented here. For our teenagers the air is turbulent and the clouds are thick. Our job is to teach them to use the values instrument panel so they can arrive safely at their destination.

What is a value? The apostle Paul described a value as what we "set our hearts on" and what we "set our minds on" (Col. 3:1–2). What we live for and think about is what we value. When we value something, we honor it, we love it, we hold it in high esteem. A value is a quality, object, or person that we look at and say, "That is important."

A book collector ran into an acquaintance to whom old books did not mean anything. In fact, he said that he had recently thrown away a big old Bible that had been in his attic for generations. Describing it, he said, "And somebody named Guten— something printed it. The book collector gasped, "Not Gutenberg. You idiot! You have thrown away one of the first books ever printed. A copy sold recently at an auction for over a million dollars." Unmoved, the other man responded, "No, not my copy. It couldn't have brought a dime. Some fellow named Luther, Martin Luther, had scribbled notes all through it."

One man's trash was another man's treasure. What one person values, another does not.

For followers of Christ, Jesus is our "core value." He is at the center of our value system because our lives are "now hidden with Christ in God" (Col. 3:3). We will fly by His "things above" instrument panel. He will keep us on course when the pressure is on to behave otherwise.

> My friend, Hani, a brilliant, young medical doctor from a Middle Eastern country shared his faith with a Moslem. (Due to the danger of being a Christian in his country, neither his real name or country can be given.) Arrested and put in prison for this, they placed Hani in a cell with another man. The cell was only large enough for the two of them to stand. Hani contracted a kidney disease and almost died. At any point he could have renounced Jesus Christ and been freed. Instead, he remained in prison almost to the point of death. Only the assassination of the country's president made it possible for him to go free. When I asked him what he learned from his prison experience, he replied, "I learned that only two things are important in life: to love God and love people." Clearly knowing his values before prison kept him from giving in to the pressure, and his prison experience served to intensify and deepen his core values.

We don't have to go to prison to discover or deepen our values. But as we "set our hearts on things above," God will focus and fashion our values around Jesus.

Vertigo Values

Flying can easily cause vertigo. Even pilots get it. Vertigo means losing all sense of where we are because we get dizzy and everything feels like it is spinning. Our culture has "vertigo values." We are spinning out of control.

Our purpose points us to our destination, but our values determine our behavior on the way.

Professor Allan Bloom, professor of social thought at the University of Chicago and author of *The Closing of the American Mind,* notes, "There is one thing a professor can be absolutely certain of: almost every student entering the university believes, or says he believes, that truth is relative."[1] Professor Bloom goes on to explain that the debunking of moral values has actually affected the intellectual ability of American students.

The debunking of moral values or "vertigo values" has left our culture out of control. We are in moral chaos. Sounding like he watched today's news, the apostle Paul addressed the issue. He gave a partial list of "vertigo values" in Colossians 3:5–9 that is appropriately situated in the context of an illustration of undressing and dressing. Just as a person takes off dirty clothes to take a bath, we need to take these off:

- sexual immorality
- impurity
- lust
- evil desires
- greed
- lying
- anger
- rage
- malice
- slander
- filthy language

These "earthly things" no longer have value to us. Do you still "wear" any of these? Take them off! Picture yourself dropping them to the floor like dirty, sweaty, stinking clothes.

VITAL VALUES

Upon landing our plane in Santa Fe on that fateful day, the pilot grinned and exclaimed, "Cheated death again." When a plane crashes, almost always it is attributed to "pilot error." If the pilot operates the plane correctly, you will get to your destination. If he doesn't, you're dead.

Our values are like that.

When we have values like the ones in Colossians 3:12–16, then those values create vitality, life, in us. Without them we become dead, lifeless. Following Paul's illustration of undressing and dressing (vv. 9–10), we see that once we get the dirty clothes off, then we put the clean clothes on. We clothe ourselves with

- compassion
- kindness
- humility
- gentleness
- patience
- forbearance
- forgiveness
- love
- peace
- thanksgiving

These "things above" have great value. Put them on! Picture yourself taking each one off the hanger and putting it on to wear. Now you are stylin', lookin' good from God's point of view.

In summary fashion Richard Halverson, former chaplain of the U.S. Senate, captured the contrast of getting rid of "vertigo values" and taking on "vital values."

> We become like what is most important in our lives.
>
> To live for pleasure is to become giddy-shallow-empty.
>
> To live for fame is to become arrogant and rude.
>
> To live for power and influence is to become thoughtless-hard-insensitive-overbearing-oppressive.
>
> To live for wealth is to become selfish-greedy-avaricious.
>
> To live for the will of God is to become selfless-loving-caring-whole.
>
> It is to become like Jesus Christ who lived to do only that which pleased His heavenly Father.[2]

Finding Congruity

"How do I determine which values I need for my life? How do I decide which ones are important?" you may ask.

> While speaking in St. Simons Island, Georgia, I met Bill, a businessman who helps the Lithuanian government buy American planes. He invited me to take a plane tour over the islands. That sounded like fun. When I met him at his office, I was expecting to take the shiny twin engine plane in the hangar. He took me out to the seven Lithuanian planes he had bought recently. He got excited about us flying one of these old "red and white tin cans" with cotton cloth bi-wings. Four of us pushed the propeller ten times to get it started. The instrument panel was in Russian. The seats looked like nailed down kitchen chairs. We flew with the back door open!
>
> When we got up, Bill let me fly. I took it down to six feet above the beach—intentionally. I loved it. It was the unique highlight of my summer. I got so excited about that little trip because I value adventure highly.

That experience brought together a value (adventure) and the application of that value (the plane ride). This is called the *principle of congruity*. That means the coming together of what you believe (a value) and how you perform (an action).[3]

We can diagram it like this.

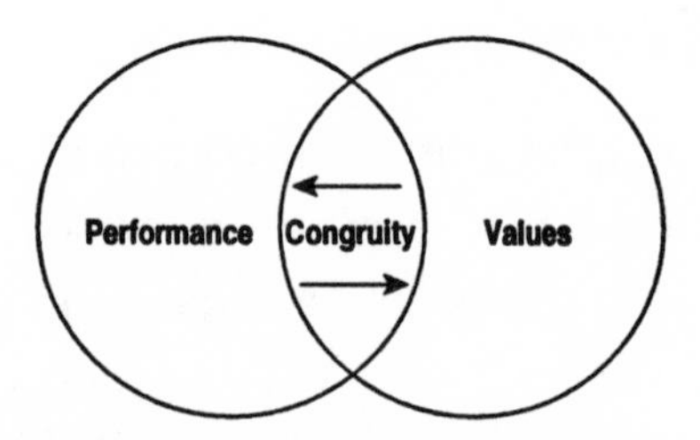

The more our values and our performance overlap, the higher the degree of congruity. The more congruity we have in our lives, the more fulfillment we have and the more we live out our destiny.

We can operate on four different levels of values, which are described below. But when our "core value" is Jesus Christ (Col. 3:3), congruity is at its highest level.

1. *Instincts.* This person lives by natural urges, seeking to satisfy base desires.
2. *Approval.* Values are determined by the approval of others—family, church, community, friends.
3. *Conscience.* Behavior adjusts to conscience. This person has a moral sense of right and wrong.
4. *Christian.* This person utilizes his conscience for guidance and the Holy Spirit to empower him or her. Here a person becomes most complete, realizing the divinely ordained potential of his or her life. Here he or she experiences the highest degree of congruity.[4]

Understanding these four levels shows us the significance of biblical values. On the Christian level not only can we know the highest values, but also we have the supernatural power to act on those values so that what we value and how we behave are in congruity. Knowing that the biggest struggle teenagers have is in getting what they believe to match up to their behavior, we can understand how vital it is to clarify these values if our whole family is going to live to reflect His glory.

Get Ready

1. Work through each step of the Values Investigation at the end of the chapter until you have clearly expressed your values in writing.
2. Verbally express those to your teenager or a friend.

   I have included an example of my values to give you a starting point for yours.

BARRY ST. CLAIR'S VALUES

Jesus Christ. Develop an intimate and intense relationship with Jesus Christ characterized by obedience.

Family. Love my family and lead them to reflect Christ to others.

People. Care for every person with the compassion of Christ, and exhibit loyalty to those closest to me.

Spirit-led Living. Release the Holy Spirit in me so that I live to reflect the fruit of the Spirit.

Leadership. Demonstrate humble servant leadership that reflects Christ, guides people into a growing relationship to Christ, and produces excellence in ministry.

Integrity. Act according to truth and purity, keeping my life clean, simple, ordered, focused, and accountable.

Helping My Teenager Get Ready

1. Ask God to help your teenager grasp what he or she values.
2. Work through the Values Investigation with your teenager. Take this in small doses so your teenager doesn't get frustrated in the process. Set aside thirty minutes each night to work on it together (or whatever blocks of time you can arrange). When the values are finalized, then enthusiastically affirm them.
3. Talk about what each of you is discovering in the process. Use the Funtalk questions.

Ask someone who does calligraphy to pen your teenager's purpose and values. Frame it and give it to your teenager as a gift when you complete the study of the book.

FUNTALK

Follow the instructions for the five points of the Values Investigation at the end of the chapter. Spend thirty minutes each night going over one of the points per work session with your teenager.

- *First night:* Let's understand the values grid on page 123. What are we trying to accomplish? (Go over the three questions under the first point in the Values Investigation clarifying what you will try to do.)
- *Second night:* Let's brainstorm possible values.
- *Third night:* Let's choose the final list of six values.
- *Fourth night:* Let's define each value as an action statement.
- *Fifth night:* Let's identify any incongruity.
  (See the example of Barry St. Clair's values if you have questions about what to do.)

PARENTS' DISCUSSION GROUP

Gather enough blank sales tags for everyone to have six. Get these from one of your local merchants. When the group assembles, give six tags to each person. Have six three-by-five-inch cards and some tape for each one also.

1. Write the key word of each of your values on the three-by-five-inch cards. You have one hundred dollars to spend. Assign a price to each value. The total amount for the six values should equal one hundred dollars. Write the price on the tag and attach the tag with tape to the card. Do this for all six values.
2. Share your six values and why you priced them as you did. (If you think time will become an issue, either create smaller groups or have only some parents share.)
3. Discuss the nightly sessions you had with your teenagers. (Let parents share any personal stories and/or the values their teenagers wrote.)
4. Pray for your teenager by name. Ask the Lord to make your teenager's values clear to him or her. Ask that your teen will live by these values throughout his or her life.

VALUES INVESTIGATION

Follow these steps to determine your values.

1. Brainstorm possible values.

   Make a list of all of your possible values. Then look through them to see if any of them could combine with others.

2. Understand the following values grid.

   Picture your values like this:

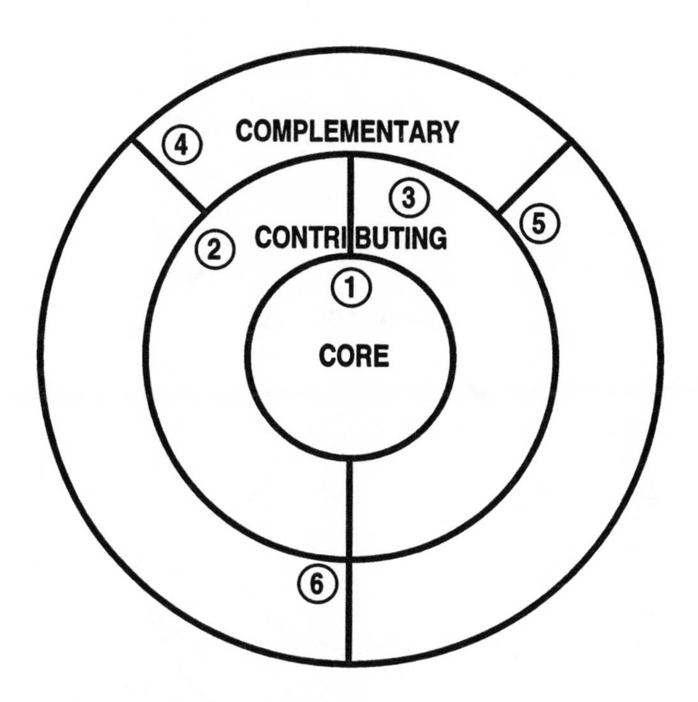

Ask yourself these questions:

- What is my core value? The most important one to you.
- What values contribute to my core value? The two values that are next most important to you.
- What values complement my first three values? The three values that you consider most important after the first three.

3. Choose your final list of six values.

   Determine the six values that you deem most important, then decide which is your core value, which two are your contributing values, and which are your complimentary values.

   1. ______________________________
   2. ______________________________
   3. ______________________________
   4. ______________________________
   5. ______________________________
   6. ______________________________

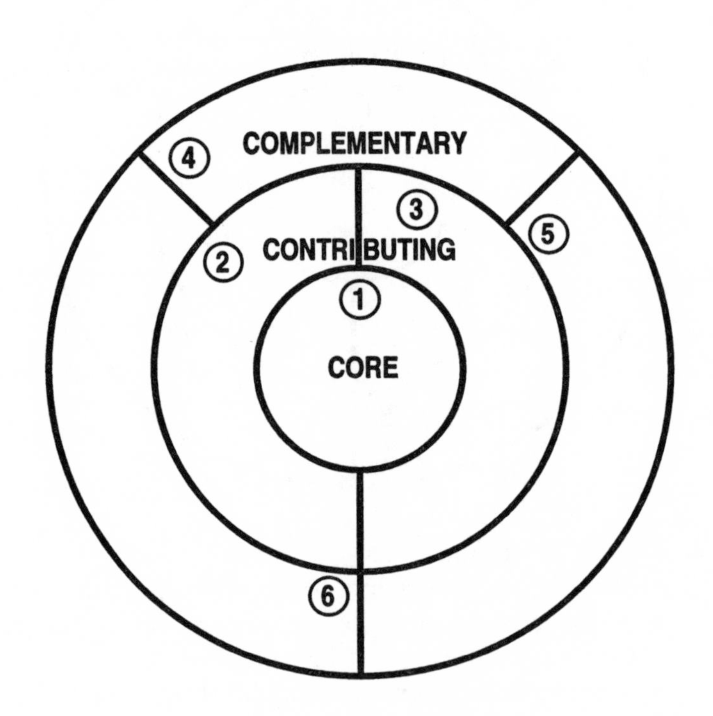

4. Define each value as an action statement.
   Begin the statement with an action verb, then define how the value will be expressed. (For example: Family. Love my family. Please them to reflect Christ to others).

   1. ______________________________
   2. ______________________________
   3. ______________________________
   4. ______________________________
   5. ______________________________
   6. ______________________________

5. Identify any incongruity.
   Write down any areas where your behavior does not match up to your values. Ask the Lord to bring your behavior in line with your values. Take whatever steps He shows you.

   ____

   ____

   ____

   ____

   ____

   ____

11 Run for the Finish Line

What are your teenager's goals, and how can he or she reach them?

Finish the Atlanta Marathon in less than three hours! To cover 26.2 miles in that time would qualify me for the Boston Marathon. Could I reach that goal?

Even before I started, I almost self-destructed. With all of my training and preparation I forgot one small detail. In all of the excitement I left my race number on the counter at home. I didn't have time to go back and get it. I called my wife, Carol. In trying to find it, she woke up everyone at 6:30 A.M. on Thanksgiving Day. The hunt was on. And they found it. By then there was no time to get it to me. The race officials told me that I could start the race without my number, but I couldn't finish without it. Whew!

My father-in-law had taken me to the race. We worked it out for him to meet me with the number at a certain point. By the time we arranged everything and I hurried to the starting line, the race had begun. Not only did I not have time to warm up, but I began the race forty-five seconds late.

With all of those glitches and distractions, I could have quit before the race began. Up to mile 20 I was ahead of my pace of 6:30 per mile and I had my number!. Then it began to rain and I "hit the wall." With shoes that felt like they weighed twenty pounds apiece, and cold rain that caused my legs to cramp, my body was yelling at me: "STOP!" Others were stopping, why didn't I? Often I've asked myself, "Why did you keep on running?" I had a goal! I didn't want to give up on my lifetime goal of running in the Boston Marathon. That caused me to press on. Using every ounce of energy I had, I finished in two hours and fifty-seven minutes. I reached the goal!

THAT SAME SORT OF FOCUSED INTENSITY is what the apostle Paul had in mind when he wrote Philippians 3:13–14: "But I've got my eye on the goal, where God is beckoning us onward—to Jesus. I'm off and running, and I'm not turning back. So let's keep focused on that goal" (THE MESSAGE).

Following Jesus is like a race—a marathon. Only those who have their goals clearly in mind will "press on toward the goal to win the prize." How do we do that?

CONNECTING WITH OUR PURPOSE

Our endless number of activities and "to do" lists cause our lives to look like this:

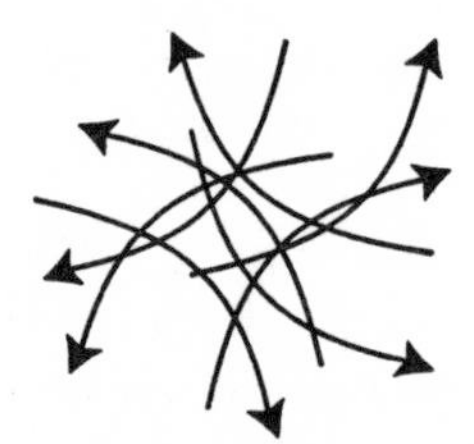

One big complaint I hear from youth pastors is that their kids are too busy. One parent of three teenagers told me last week: "By the time we get to the weekend my kids are so exhausted that they sleep half the day, and then they sit around staring into space. They are pooped from the pace." Someone called this "the barrenness of busyness." The results are not only that our families are exhausted but that we do lots of good things that keep us from doing God's best things. When we learn to set goals that connect to our purpose and teach our teenagers how to as well, then we can either avoid the "pooped pace" or we can know why we are running that fast.

Every goal we set, large or small, should move us toward our life purpose.

Mike Philips starts us down the road to solving the problem: "There's a lot of verbal 'fog' floating around in Christian circles because of fuzzy ill-defined purposes and goals. We talk about giving God glory, taking the gospel into the world, and living God-honoring lives. But as long as such statements remain undefined, they are useless."[1]

When we set goals that connect to our life purpose and values, we can be confident that every decision is taking us in the right direction. Then our lives can look like this:

That's exactly what the apostle Paul had in mind when he said, "But I press on to take hold of that for which Christ Jesus took hold of me" (Phil. 3:12).

In order to run the race we, like Paul, must "take hold of" goals that move us toward our purpose. For years I knew this must be true, but I didn't know how to make that connection. Now I know, and I want to show you so you can do this successfully and so you can teach your teenagers to do it. This is a vital link to your destiny and theirs.

Our Need to Achieve

Struggling with reaching his purpose and goals, the apostle Paul made a confession: "I do not consider myself yet to have taken hold of it . . . . I press on toward the goal" (Phil. 3:13–14).

Most people struggle with setting goals. We seem to fall into one of two ditches on the road to goal setting.

Hyper goal setters. Carried away with changing the world by the end of this week, hyper goal setters set themselves on a burnout course. Unrealistic and inflexible goals dull their sensitivity to people. Driving overachievers quickly get their lives out of balance.

Non-goal setters. Not wanting to get out of their comfort zone, non-goal setters don't see the need for setting goals. Satisfied with the status quo, they don't like to be challenged to press on. They like their lives just like they are.

Some of us may be stalled on the side of the road for other reasons:

- No one has shown me the importance of goal setting.
- I don't know how to approach it.
- I don't like to write things down.
- It is too much trouble.
- I haven't taken the time.
- I failed in the past and feel I would never reach the goal.

Whatever the reason, we miss out on the balance that God desires. Each personality type will respond to goal setting differently. We need to approach this carefully with our teenagers, allowing them to set goals according to their personality, not ours. However, we can say with biblical certainty that God desires everyone to enter into balanced goal setting in order to achieve God's purpose for our lives. We must set goals if we are going to "win the prize."

Ari Kiev, associate professor of psychiatry at Cornell University, clarifies that need for us.

> I have repeatedly found that helping people to develop personal goals has proved to be the most effective way to help them cope with problems and help them maximize their satisfaction. Observing the lives of people who have mastered adversity, I have repeatedly noted that they have established goals and, irrespective of obstacles, sought with all their effort to achieve them. From the moment they fixed an objective in their mind and decided to concentrate all their energies on a specific goal, they began to surmount the most difficult odds.[2]

When we set goals and help our children to do so, we benefit for many reasons.[3]

1. *We avoid the tyranny of the urgent.* Without goals, daily urgencies overwhelm us so that we rarely get to the really important things. Charles Hummel explains what happens to us.

   > We live in constant tension between the urgent and the important. The problem is that the important task rarely must be done today . . . . But the urgent tasks call for urgent action—endless demands; pressure every hour and day . . . we realize we have become slaves to the tyranny of the urgent.[4]

2. *We get revitalized.* People with goals generally have tremendous energy reserves. They create energy as they set systematic goals that move them toward their life purpose.
3. *We accomplish more.* Only three percent of all people have goals written down. Ten percent more have them in their heads.

Eighty-seven percent drift through life with no definite goals. The three percent accomplish fifty to one hundred times more in their lifetimes than those ten percent who have the goals in their heads. And they achieve infinitely more than those who have no goals.[5]

4. *We experience fulfillment.* Personally, I have discovered that almost every time I get discouraged I can trace it to having lost sight of my goals or having too many goals. One of the outstanding benefits of setting goals is personal happiness. Mack Douglas says: "One of the outstanding benefits of goals is personal happiness. Life is too short to be unhappy. But you will never be happy until you are achieving a worthy, challenging goal."[6]
5. *We build confidence.* Without goals we don't know how to proceed. Like walking in a dark room, we run into walls and hit our shins. We get confused about where we are and where we are supposed to go. Goal setting turns the light on so we can see to move through the room with confidence.

My dad epitomized the results of these benefits.

> At seventy my dad retired, sort of. He dreamed about buying some land on the interstate to build a motel. He didn't need the money, the hassle, or something else to do. But he felt like God gave him the vision for it and the ability to do it. So he borrowed the money, purchased the land, got the construction crew, and built a motel. He had never been in the motel business before! Why did he build it? He had a dream, a goal. Even past seventy years old, he never stifled his need to achieve—to press on toward the goal.

Concentration on Specifics

Dawson Trotman, founder of the Navigators, coined "This one thing I do; not forty things I dabble at" from the apostle Paul's expression "but one thing I do" (Phil. 3:13). David Schwartz sheds more light on this idea when he says: "A goal is more than a dream; it is a dream being acted upon. It is more than a lazy "Oh, I wish I could . . . ." A goal is a clear "This is what I'm working toward.'"[7]

How do we set specific goals that move us toward our purpose? Think about one goal you want to accomplish. Get it clearly in your mind. Write it in the space below.

___

___

___

Now ask yourself these twelve questions to see if you have set an appropriate goal.

1. *Do I understand what a goal is?* According to Webster a goal is "an end that one strives for." The goal is the finish line.
2. *Have I written the goal?* Since we remember only 10 percent of what we hear but retain 70 percent of what we hear and write, it makes sense that our goals will be clearer if we write them. Writing keeps it before us to remind us where we are headed.
3. *Have I set the right goal?* Disappointment results when we set the wrong goals. A wrong goal satisfies our own selfish desires, leaving God and others out of the picture. But setting the right goal and achieving it honors God and others. We can ask ourselves, "Does this goal please the Lord?"
4. *Is this God's goal for me?* Praying through the goal allows us to determine if the goal fits our purpose and values. Imagine how much time, energy, and effort we can save by only pursuing God's goals.
5. *Is my goal big enough?* Dawson Trotman gave a profound challenge, "Why pray for peanuts when God wants to give us continents?" Small goals stifle our faith, our vision, and our walk with Christ. Let's allow our goals to stretch our faith. Let's dream big dreams—big enough that unless God comes through we are doomed to failure.
6. *Have I established a realistic goal?* On the flip side we have to ask ourselves if the goal is doable. No one can be an astronaut if he has never been to college. Or to bring it closer to home, a person cannot get an A in a course if she has not cracked a book all semester. Unrealistic goals overwhelm and demotivate us. Yet realistic goals set within realistic time frames bring success.
7. *Can I visualize the goal?* Picture yourself reaching your goal. What do you see? Is it worth achieving? Visualizing the goal will program your subconscious mind so that your actions will follow what your mind has seen. Right thinking always precedes right acting.

8. *Have I committed myself to the goal?* Ask yourself: "In light of other goals, can I realistically commit myself to this particular goal?"
9. *What barriers do I face?* Every worthy goal will face obstacles. The more lofty our goals, the greater the obstacles. But we will willingly jump over these hurdles when we know that we are pursuing God's goals. Allow for obstacles without getting discouraged and quitting.
10. *Have I broken down the goal into simple, reachable steps?* The old adage goes, "How do you eat an elephant? One bite at a time." We won't accomplish the goal all in one day. But we need to do something to reach it every day. We need to break our goals into bite-sized chunks?
11. *Who will hold me accountable for this goal?* People live sloppy lives when no one holds them accountable. But when we are accountable, we help each other set goals, keep on track, and feel encouraged when we want to quit.
12. *When do I set other goals?* We find time to do what is important to us. Carve out a few hours one afternoon or a few minutes every day over the next week to write your goals.

The Prize

The result? The "prize."

> When I finished the marathon, the officials put a medal around my neck—the prize. I had qualified to run the Boston Marathon. (That's another story.)

When we finish life's race, having pursued God's goals for us, He will place around our necks "the prize." Like Paul we will be able to say, "I have fought the good fight, I have finished the race, . . . Now there is in store for me the crown of righteousness" (2 Tim. 4:7–8).

As wonderful as that is, every Christian parent desires that their children would be able to say the same thing. As they learn to set God's goals for their lives, they too will get "the prize"!

GET READY

1. Write your goals using the outlines on page 136.
    - Set at least one goal under each category. Make each one personal (yours not somebody elses); practical (realistic); and measurable (specific).
    - Under each goal write down the steps you'll need to take to help you get there.
    - Set your Lifetime Goals, then refer to them to set your One Year Goals. Then use your One Year Goals to set your Monthly Goals.
    - Take plenty of time to work on this. Don't feel like you have to finish it all in one week. Write your goals. Obviously this will take more than the time you have for this week. Work on your Lifetime Goals this week, then your One Year Goals next week and so on.

2. Verbally express your goals to your teenager, spouse, or a friend.

   Included here is an example of one of my goals to give you encouragement in setting yours.

    - Lifetime Goal: As a husband, I will meet Carol's needs by understanding her and loving her, and praying with her and for her.
    - One Year Goal: To have three getaway weekends this year with Carol for personal, spiritual refreshment.
    - Monthly Goal: Give Carol 3 days this month to work on family issues, to give her time to work on her Hebrews course and for our personal getaway.

HELPING MY TEENAGER GET READY

1. Ask God to help your teenager catch the significance of writing goals.
2. Work through the Goal Setting Exercise with your teen-ager. Like the Values Evaluation in chapter 10, take this in small steps so your teenager doesn't get frustrated. Set aside thirty minutes each night to work on it together. When the goals are finalized, then enthusiastically affirm them.
3. Talk about what each of you is discovering in the process. Use the Funtalk questions.

Funtalk

Set aside thirty minutes each night to work on goals.

1. In your opinion what is the value of setting goals? Why do you think it is important to write them down?
2. Obviously this will take more than the time you have for this week. Let's limit ourselves to our Lifetime Goals this week. We'll get started on our One Year Goals if we have time.

    - *First night:* Spiritual goals
    - *Second night:* Mental goals
    - *Third night:* Physical goals
    - *Fourth night:* Social goals
    - *Fifth night:* Family goals and job/financial goals

3. Let's pray for each other about several specific goals we have written tonight, and let's ask God to help us reach them.

Parents' Discussion Group

Bring a dart board to the group. Also bring a small prize for the winner.

1. Have each person in the group take a turn at darts. Determine the winner by who gets closest to the bull's-eye. Give the winner the prize. Now blindfold two contestants, spin them around, and have them toss the darts. Point out that when we take aim with focused goals we are much more likely to hit the target.
2. What did you struggle with the most in trying to write your goals? Why?
3. Share your Lifetime Goals. (If you think time will become an issue, either let them share in smaller groups or let as many share as time will allow.)
4. Discuss how you did with the nightly sessions with your teenager. (Let parents share any personal stories and/or the goals their teenagers set.)
5. Talk about how to continue this process by setting One Year Goals and Monthly Goals over the next two weeks.
6. Pray for your teenager by name. Ask the Lord to make his or her goals clear, and ask the Lord to help your teenager reach his or her goals.

GOAL SETTING EXERCISE

LIFETIME GOALS

(Luke 2:52)

- Spiritual (quiet time, prayer, Bible study, accountability/discipleship, outreach, church, ministry)
- Mental (reading, planning, studying)
- Physical (exercise, diet, sleep)
- Social (friends, activities)
- Family (spouse, children, parents, brothers and sisters)
- Job/Finances (hours worked, money earned, possessions, tithe)

GOAL SETTING EXERCISE

One Year Goals

(Luke 2:52)

- Spiritual (quiet time, prayer, Bible study, accountability/ discipleship, outreach, church, ministry)
- Mental (reading, planning, studying)
- Physical (exercise, diet, sleep)
- Social (friends, activities)
- Family (spouse, children, parents, brothers and sisters)
- Job/Finances (hours worked, money earned, possessions, tithe)

GOAL SETTING EXERCISE

Monthly Goals

(Luke 2:52)

- Spiritual (quiet time, prayer, Bible study, accountability/ discipleship, outreach, church, ministry)
- Mental (reading, planning, studying)
- Physical (exercise, diet, sleep)
- Social (friends, activities)
- Family (spouse, children, parents, brothers and sisters)
- Job/Finances (hours worked, money earned, possessions, tithe)

12 Watch the Clock

What time does your teenager have, and how does he or she use it?

Seventh grade PE. Basketball, dodgeball, tumbling, and running. Anything was better than classes with books, even though our gym didn't have a shower. But one activity I hated—rope climbing. Gripping the rope tightly with my hands then wrapping my feet around the rope, I would start to climb. With hand over fist pushing against the law of gravity, I felt the strength go out of my arms. When I checked my progress, I had only climbed eight feet and had twenty to go. I couldn't do it. One day, after repeated efforts, I made it. I got so excited when I touched the top that I slid down quickly, letting the rope run through my fingers. When I reached the floor, my hands looked like one big, raw, juicy blister.

OUR STRUGGLE WITH TIME PARALLELS that rope climb. Getting time under control is like the constant strain of pulling up on the rope. Yet just at the point when we conquer it, like a slick rope, it slides through our fingers.

Time, unlike money, cannot be saved, only spent. No saving for a rainy day, we must spend every second now. Yesterday is a canceled check. Tomorrow is a promissory note. Today must be spent wisely.[1]

Every night at dinner we used to have six people sitting around the table. Now we have only four. Two have left the nest. It seems like only yesterday that we brought them home from the hospital. We say, "My how time flies." And it does. Soon our teenagers will be gone. That is why this discussion is so significant for us as parents. Not only do we need to use our time wisely in the general sense, but also we need to use it wisely specifically in building our relationships with our kids.

My friend Dave has a son the same age as my son. Dave's son played basketball this year (or didn't play would be more accurate). But Dave was there for his son. Every game. Lots of practices. Many late nights, after the game, crying times. "We hurt together," Dave said, "and we bonded." Dave got into his son's world. That takes mega-time. Was it worth it? You bet!

We need to consider seriously whether we are spending our time wisely.

And our teenagers—that's a tougher nut to crack. Zip! Zip! They're here. They're gone. Getting that license changes everything. The fact that they work with you on this book every week is a huge step in the right direction for them. Have you noticed? They are always busy. Yet they have large chunks of time to do what they want to do. Our job is not to make them more or less busy, but to help them find balance. How can we help them use their time in a way that reflects their goals and values and moves them toward their life purpose?

The average American who lives seventy years spends his or her time like this:

- 23 years sleeping
- 19 years working
- 9 years playing
- 6 years traveling
- 6 years eating
- 4 years sick
- 2 years dressing
- 1 year in church

We spend 69/70ths of life on temporal things and only 1/70th pursuing our eternal destiny.

Time is ticking by. To understand how to use it wisely, picture a clock with three hands ticking. When we understand how these three hands work, we will know how to use our time and how to help our teenagers use their time to pursue our destiny.

Contrasting wisdom and foolishness in Ephesians 5:15–17, the apostle Paul told us how to use the three ticking hands to watch the clock: "Be very careful, then, how you live—not as unwise but as wise, making the most of every opportunity, because the days are evil. Therefore do not be foolish, but understand what the Lord's will is."

The Hour Hand—Look At How You Live

Ephesians 5:15 can read, "Look at how you conduct your life and spend your time." We can do that best by contrasting how we look at time with how God looks at it.

The White Rabbit

We approach time like the white rabbit in Lewis Carroll's *Alice in Wonderland.* Always in a hurry, the white rabbit would pull out his watch and pop down a hole whenever Alice tried to get close to him. Running away from himself and others, he would exclaim, "Oh my ears and whiskers, how late it is getting!" Like the white rabbit we find ourselves always in a hurry. Sometimes we are running away from ourselves and our relationships. Sometimes our circumstances force us into an out-of-breath use of time.

William Elliot put this problem in perspective for us: "The reason why so many of us are overwrought, tense, distracted and anxious is that we have never mastered the art of living one day at a time . . . mentally we live in all three tenses at once—past, present and future . . . . And that will not work! 'The load of tomorrow, added to that of yesterday, carried today make the strongest falter.'"[2]

The Time Monster

Even though we panic about time, we waste tremendous amounts of it. "Where did all of my time go?" we wonder. The "Time Monster" seems to steal time from us.

Looking at this list, circle your top three time wasters in each category.[3]

SELF-IMPOSED	OTHERS IMPOSED
Procrastination	Interruptions
Indecision	Meetings
Misplaced items	Telephone
Junk mail	Family problems
Television	Poor communication
Lack of goals	Ineffective help
Lack of planning	Role not clear
Preoccupation	Shifting priorities
Ineffective delegation	Drop-in visitors
Wrong priorities	Waiting for people
Failure to listen	Commuting time

Emotional upset	Negative attitudes
Poor organization	Detail work
Lack of self-discipline	Overlong visits

Timing Is Everything

By contrast, when we look at the clock from God's perspective, we find a much different approach than either panic or waste.

1. *Life is brief.* Get God's insight on the brevity of life from Psalm 39:4–5.

   Show me, O Lord, my life's end and the number of my days;
   let me know how fleeting is my life.
   You have made my days a mere handbreadth;
   the span of my years is as nothing before you.
   Each man's life is but a breath.

2. *Use time wisely.* The Scriptures points out that there is a direct correlation between the use of our time and wisdom: "Teach us to number our days aright, that we may gain a heart of wisdom" (Ps. 90:12).
3. *Accomplish your destiny.* God will give us enough time to accomplish everything within our destiny. "There is a time for everything, and a season for every activity under heaven" (Eccl. 3:1).

Neither panic nor waste are options for us because "He [God] has made everything beautiful in its time" (Eccl. 3:11).

Timing is everything! But only when it is in God's hands. Not only does He control the tick of the clock, the writer of Ecclesiastes went so far as to say that "He has . . . set eternity in the hearts of men" (Eccl. 3:11). With the time He has given us, He will accomplish His purpose for us.

Because we choose God's perspective we can pray this prayer.

Slow me down, Lord!
Ease the pounding of my heart by the quieting of my mind.
Give me, amid the confusion of the day, a calmness of the everlasting hills.
Break the tension of my nerves and muscles with the soothing music of the singing streams that live in my memory. Help me to know the magical, restoring power of sleep.

Teach me the art of taking minute vacations—of slowing down to look at a flower, to chat with a friend, to pat a dog, to read a few lines from a good book.
Remind me each day of the fable of the hare and the tortoise, that I may know that the race is not always to the swift—that there is more to life than increasing its speed.
Let me look upward into the branches of the towering oak and know that it grew great and strong because it grew slowly and well.
Slow me down, Lord, and inspire me to send my roots deep into the soil of life's enduring values that I may grow toward the stars of my great destiny.
In Jesus' name, Amen.

(Author unknown. "Slow Me Down, Lord")

The Minute Hand—Make Every Minute Count

When the apostle Paul wrote of "making the most of every opportunity" (Eph. 5:16), he gave us the minute hand on the clock.

Through this verse we find two great ideas about how to use time wisely.

1. *Make every minute count.* Let's picture ourselves in the grocery store filling a cart with our favorite food. The same principle applies to time: putting into every minute the best stuff we can.
2. *Redeem the time.* After I eat at one of my favorite fast-food restaurants so many times using my frequent diner card, I can redeem it for a free meal. If we use our time for God's purposes, He will redeem it. He will multiply our use of time for His glory.

The greatest example of making every minute count and redeeming the time was Jesus. It was no coincidence that He had completed His life's mission by age thirty-three. Even though He had a brief life span, He was never in a hurry, in a panic, or burned out. Because of the quality of the way He spent His time, He didn't need as much quantity to fulfill His destiny. Because Jesus lives in us, we can have that same balanced approach, no matter how long we live on this earth.

No one has any more or less time each day than anyone else. It's all in the way we choose to use it. Each one of us has 1440 minutes a day, 168 hours a week. Of those hours we will:

sleep	56 hours
eat and dress	20 hours
work	40 hours
travel	8 hours
TOTAL	124 hours
OPTIONAL	44 hours

What could we do with 44 hours a week used wisely? Mike Philips says, "The distinction between a successful and mediocre existence is in those surplus minutes and hours which are either frittered away or afforded miserly care."[5] Make every minute count!

THE SECOND HAND—CONTROL THE TIME

By now we know we need to make adjustments in the use of our time. Paul's letter to the Ephesians helps us again: "Do not be foolish, but understand what the Lord's will is. Do not get drunk on wine, which leads to debauchery. Instead, be filled with the Spirit" (Eph. 5:17–18).

Fools, like the drunk in verse 18, are out of control. Because they squander what they have, they miss out on God's will for their lives. On the other hand, the wise who are controlled by the Spirit make prudent decisions about the use of their resources, including time. Because of that, they walk in God's will.

Dr. Howard Hendricks hammers this point home:

> "The older . . . I become in the faith, the more impressed I am that the management of my time is the greatest barometer of my control by the Spirit. If you really want to know if you are under the control of the Spirit, evaluate your use of the time God has given to you . . . . The fruit of the Spirit includes self-control."[6]

When we live under the Spirit's control we allow Him to discipline our use of time.

How do we take a giant step toward making wise time decisions?

Say no graciously.

"I am convinced that the most difficult word to pronounce is not Zaanannim (Josh. 19:33) or Hazzelelponi (1 Chron. 4:3). This word is even harder to say than 'The sixth sick sheik's sixth sheep is sick'. The word . . . is 'no.'"[7]

Charles Spurgeon said it more directly: "Learn to say no; it will be more use to you than to be able to read Latin. When you don't say no you make promises you can't keep, go to meetings that are not necessary and waste time in many inappropriate activities."[8]

Saying no is tough! We want people to like us. We think the need is urgent. We think we are indispensable. "It can't be done without me." But we must remember: Every time we say no to one thing we can say yes to something else!

Let's do all we can to teach our teenagers not to let time slip through their fingers. And more importantly, let's not let it slip through our teenager's fingers. They think they will live forever. As we teach them to value and use time, then both of us can use it to climb the rope to our goals, our purpose, and ultimately to God's destiny for our lives.

Get Ready

1. Pray the "Slow Me Down, Lord" prayer every day this week.
2. Go through the **TIME EXERCISE** on page 147. Make sure you have completed your purpose and goals first, so that they tie into your time decisions.
3. Spend quality time on the **TIME EXERCISE** with your teenager. Agree to hold each other accountable for the use of your time.

Helping My Teenager Get Ready

NOTE: These steps will take more than one week to implement, so be patient and don't quit. It will pay off!

1. Ask God to help your teenager see the significance of scheduling time and of going through the discipline of connecting his or her goals with his or her schedule.
2. Work through the **TIME EXERCISE** with your teenager. Set aside thirty minutes each night, or as much time as you can get, to work on it together.
3. Talk about what each of you is discovering in the process. Use the Funtalk questions.

Offer to pay for a calendar/planning system for your teenager. Be sure he or she really intends to use the system before you invest the money. Decide together what you will order and follow through.

FUNTALK

Set aside thirty minutes each night to work on the Time Exercise.

- *First night:* Once we get our schedules connected to our goals what do you think will be the benefits? Together decide what kind of calendar/planning system you want and order it. If you buy it locally or get it shipped overnight, you will have it to work on immediately.
- *Second night:* Let's look at each other's Time Log and identify the three places we waste the most time.
- *Third night:* Let's pull out our monthly goals and from those write out our Ideal Schedule and a To Do list.
- *Fourth night:* Let's review the Ideal Schedule and To Do list and start putting that on the calendar.
- *Fifth night:* Let's finish up all the loose ends.

Let's check all the exercises we have completed.

- ❑ Purpose completed
- ❑ Values completed
- ❑ Lifetime Goals completed
- ❑ Yearly Goals completed
- ❑ Monthly Goals completed
- ❑ Time Log completed
- ❑ Ideal Schedule completed
- ❑ Calendar started

If all of this is not completed, note that you have two more weeks to work on it before we finish the book.

Use the last few minutes each night praying together about your time.

PARENTS' DISCUSSION GROUP

1. Looking at your Time Log, where do you waste the most time?
2. What three biggest changes do you need to make to use your time more wisely?
3. Give one example of how your Ideal Schedule reflects your monthly goals.
4. Discuss how you did with the nightly sessions with your teenager. (Let parents share any personal stories and/or the struggles they have had with this.)

5. Talk about how to complete the process if any of them are not through yet. Encourage them that this is not a static but a dynamic process that probably will need more time to complete. Motivate them to keep working on it.
6. Pray for your teenager by name. Ask the Lord to help him or her to use his or her time wisely so that every minute will count for the glory of God.

TIME EXERCISE

To use your time most wisely, take these steps.

1. To observe accurately how you live, fill out the Time Log on page 149 for one week. It will help you know with accuracy where your time is going now. You will be surprised!
2. To make every minute count, fill out the Ideal Schedule on page 150. The Ideal Schedule should reflect your monthly goals.

Fill in the Ideal Schedule by looking back over your monthly goals. Place each monthly goal into the schedule or otherwise you are not purposefully pursuing that goal.

For example, if one of my Lifetime Goals is "To experience increasing intimacy with Jesus Christ," my One Year Goal is "To spend time alone with God daily," and my One Month Goal is "To spend thirty minutes in prayer and Bible study every day," then I fill that in on my calendar for thirty minutes every day.

Fill in the entire schedule including time to rest and relax. That way you plan your time rather than others planning it for you. That does not mean you are selfish or exclude other people. But it does indicate that you have a prepared strategy for making every minute count with God, others, and yourself.

3. To control the time, order a calendar/planning system at an office supply store. One such option is the Daytimer, which can be ordered from

Daytimer Inc.
Allentown, PA 18601
(215) 395-5884

We need the proper tools for planning in the same way we need a lawnmower for cutting the grass. A tool like the Daytimer gives an opportunity to record our schedules and notes in one place and have it before us every day. This tool is critical when we put our monthly goals into our schedule.

4. When your calendar arrives, go through each day of the month putting in your Ideal Schedule each week. Then make certain that every monthly goal is either on the schedule or on your daily To Do list.

To make sure you are doing first things first, prioritize your To Do list. At the end of the day, if you have completed only your first priority, you can rest assured you have done the most important thing.

As you turn these steps into habits, you build confidence each day that you are accomplishing your goals, your purpose, and ultimately your destiny.

DAILY TIME LOG

	Sunday	Monday	Tuesday	Wednesday	Thursday	Friday	Saturday
6:00							
6:30							
7:00							
7:30							
8:00							
8:30							
9:00							
9:30							
10:00							
10:30							
11:00							
11:30							
12:00							
12:30							
1:00							
1:30							
2:00							
2:30							
3:00							
3:30							
4:00							
4:30							
5:00							
5:30							
6:00							
6:30							
7:00							
7:30							
8:00							
8:30							
9:00							
9:30							
10:00							
10:30							
11:00							
11:30							

IDEAL TIME SCHEDULE

	Sunday	Monday	Tuesday	Wednesday	Thursday	Friday	Saturday
6:00							
6:30							
7:00							
7:30							
8:00							
8:30							
9:00							
9:30							
10:00							
10:30							
11:00							
11:30							
12:00							
12:30							
1:00							
1:30							
2:00							
2:30							
3:00							
3:30							
4:00							
4:30							
5:00							
5:30							
6:00							
6:30							
7:00							
7:30							
8:00							
8:30							
9:00							
9:30							
10:00							
10:30							
11:00							
11:30							

13 Warp and Weft 'Em

What decisions does your teenager need to make, and how can he or she make them?

Marcia weaves. When she explained how she weaves, I was totally fascinated. "I hold in my hand many strands of yarn. Then I place those longer strands on the warp. They will run the length of the fabric. When I place in other threads that run the other direction, it is called the weft. As they cross over and under, they give the fabric color and design. I can put in strong threads or weak ones. I can weave it tightly or loosely. Each of those decisions determines what the fabric will look like when I have finished."

MAKING DECISIONS PARALLELS MARCIA'S weaving. We hold the yarn of our decisions in our hands. When we make a decision, it is like placing the strands of yarn on the loom. Those decisions warp and weft to become the fabric of our lives.

Most teenagers think their decisions have no consequences. But as parents we know better. Between the ages of sixteen and twenty-six our kids make the decisions that cause them to experience the most dramatic and permanent changes in their lives. Dr. James Dobson says, "Most of the decisions that will shape the next fifty years will be made in this era, including the choice of occupation, perhaps the decision to marry, and the establishment of values and principles by which life will be governed. What makes this period even more significant is the impact of early mistakes and errors in judgment. They can undermine all that is to follow."[1]

The very thought of this frightens us as parents. We would give anything to make our teenagers' decisions for them. (And some of us are still trying!) But we know that is not right, nor healthy, nor even possible. Yet we can guide them and teach them to know how to make their own decisions and to do so wisely. In the process of their warping and wefting they create a fabric that may not be perfect, but is rich, beautiful, and unique.

As Marcia continued teaching me about weaving, she said, "In order to know what the final product will look like, I must have a 'draft.' A draft is the formula for making the pattern. Then using the treadle, the pedal that makes the pattern, and the headle, the gadget that picks up the threads, I weave the fabric to match the pattern."

Decisions do not stand alone. Rather, they are woven into the very fabric of our lives. When we understand that the decisions we make make us, we see not only the significance of every decision we make, but also the value of a "draft," a plan for our decision making.

From Philippians 2:3–13 let's develop the acrostic **DECIDE** as our "draft" to help us and our teenagers make wise decisions.

DISCERN OUR ATTITUDE

The initial "fork in the road" on any decision is our attitude. When we make a decision, we have one of two attitudes according to Philippians 2:3–5. "Do nothing out of selfish ambition or vain conceit, but in humility consider others better than yourselves. Each of you should look not only to your own interests, but also to the interests of others. Your attitude should be the same as that of Christ Jesus."

1. *A selfish attitude.* Am I making this decision to get what I want?
2. *A servant attitude.* Am I making this decision to do what Jesus wants even if I don't get what I want?

These two broad categories give us two containers in which to put every decision.

I want to buy a car. What is the first step I take in making that decision? Not cost, model, or color; but motive; attitude. Why am I buying a car?

Decisive question: Will this decision serve me or serve Christ?

EXALT JESUS AS THE LORD

Next, we want Jesus to rule over every detail of the decision-making process. How did that work in Jesus' relationship with His Father? As Jesus humbled Himself, God, in turn, exalted Him to the highest place and made Him Lord over every person and every thing (Phil. 2:6–11).

Jesus is going to be Lord no matter what decision we make. But when we humble ourselves and acknowledge that He is Lord, then we have the incredible privilege of living under His lordship. He will show us what He desires, and He will guide us to make the decision wisely.

We can easily get ahead of ourselves in the decision-making process. We must stop and remember what Proverbs 16:9 says, "In his heart a man plans his course, but the Lord determines his steps."

What car would I buy? A fast, hot, red, convertible sports car! But that's before I consider money.

Who knows, maybe God wants to give me a car! He may want me to buy a used one. Maybe He wants me to walk. Or He may want to protect me from buying a certain one.

I had the check ready to buy the car. But I told the Lord: "If for any reason you don't want us to have this, show me and I won't buy it." When I took it to my mechanic to check it out, he discovered that it had been in a severe wreck that had bent the frame! We didn't get that car! Submitting that decision to the Lord saved us mega-hassles and untold dollars.

Decisive question: Is this decision based on what Jesus desires?

Choose to Obey

Our next logical step is to obey what God tells us to do.

The apostle Paul challenged us: "As you have always obeyed . . . continue . . . " (Phil. 2:12).

To grasp the word *obeyed,* picture someone in a house who hears a rap at the door. That person goes to the door and opens it. He responds. She obeys. Done often enough that becomes a habit, a lifestyle. When we choose to obey God, then each decision builds a habit until obedience becomes a lifestyle.

Obedience removes the possibility of making a decision based on

- impulse
- impatience
- feelings
- frustrations
- disappointment
- people's expectations
- pressure

We were willing not to buy a car and walk if that was what the Lord had in mind.

We had to start back at square one after not getting the wrecked car. We felt frustrated and disappointed. The pressure was building to buy because our mechanic promised that our old car was not long for this world. What I wanted to say was, "Lord, I want a car now!" But instead I said, "Lord, I choose to obey so I can have your exact plan for the car."

Decisive question: Am I choosing to obey?

IMPLEMENT THE STEPS

The next step in making a decision calls for working through the decision-making process using the **STEPS** approach.

When Paul, the apostle, wrote "continue to work out your salvation" (Phil. 2:12), he had in mind to work out every detailed decision to the finish. This verse is not about earning our salvation by works, but rather it refers to the ongoing process of making Christlike decisions once we have salvation.

We make those decisions by working through a practical, five-step process. We can use this process to buy a car, decide which cereal to eat for breakfast, decide who to marry, or settle any other decision we make.[2]

S*ee the goal clearly.* Focus on your goal. Ask the Lord to make the goal clear based on His promise in Proverbs 2:6, "For the Lord gives wisdom, and from his mouth come knowledge and understanding." In order to avoid confusion later, write down your goal.

T*ake in the facts.* Thoroughly analyze the situation, getting all the facts before you. Ask the "who, what, where, when, why" questions. Seriously consider the challenge of Proverbs 18:13, "What a shame—yes, how stupid!—to decide before knowing the facts!" (TLB). So you will have a firm grip on the facts, write them down.

E*valuate the alternatives.* Explore all of the creative alternatives. The writer of Proverbs encouraged this openness in Proverbs 18:15, "The intelligent man is always open to new ideas. In fact, he looks for them" (TLB). Outline all of the possible alternatives.

P*roject strengths and weaknesses.* To determine the positives and negatives of the various alternatives, use the **SWOT** approach.

> **S***trengths.* What are the strengths about this alternative?
> **W***eaknesses.* What are the weaknesses about this alternative?
> **O***pportunities.* What opportunities does this provide for the future?
> **T***hreats.* What threats does this create for the future?
>
> Write out the strengths, weaknesses, opportunities, and threats for each alternative.

S*elect the best alternative.* Prayerfully select the alternative that emerges as the best one. The Lord will direct you on the basis of His promise in Proverbs 3:5–6:

> *Trust in the Lord with all your heart*
> *and lean not on your own understanding;*
> *in all your ways acknowledge him,*
> *and he will make your paths straight.*

Write down your decision in one sentence.

> We set aside all day Saturday to go through these **STEPS** We focused on the kind of car we needed. Then we went to several dealers to get the facts, taking lots of notes. We narrowed it down to two dealers who had the same car. Before we decided we put one car on one page and the other on another page, going through **SWOT** After that the decision was easy. We got a much newer, nicer car than we had ever imagined!

Decisive question: Am I using **STEPS** to think through the decision?

Delight in the Decision

We can relax with the confidence that we have made the best possible decision. Philippians 2:13 tells us why: "For God is at work in you, both to will and to work for his good pleasure" (RSV).

If He gets a kick out of us making the right decision, then certainly we can enjoy it too. At this point we get to experience the fulfillment of His promise in Psalm 37:4, "Delight yourself in the Lord and he will give you the desires of your heart."

> When, finally, we bought our car, we were delighted. We trusted the Lord through these steps. He not only protected us from "the wreck"; He provided His very best for us. In fact, the car He provided was so good we wondered if the dealer lost money on us!

Decisive Question: Am I enjoying this decision?

Evaluate with Tests

Let's say we follow this process, but the decision is still not clear. Or we make what appears to be an unwise decision. Our destiny does not hinge on making every decision correctly. We will make mistakes. God uses even our wrong decisions in the process of working out His salvation in us. He weaves that dark yarn into the fabric to make the overall design more beautiful. We learn and grow from the experience.

But how can we check our decision to evaluate if it is the right one?

> F. B. Meyer told about a large ship that navigated into a narrow harbor at night. The captain could easily have run the

> ship aground, but he never did. He always got the ship into the harbor. Asked how he did it, he replied that when the five lights in the harbor lined up in a straight line, then he knew he could turn the ship into the channel.

These five lights will help us evaluate our decisions.

1. *The communication test.* We need to talk to God seriously about this decision. *Have I listened intently to hear His answer?*
2. *The conscience test.* With the Holy Spirit living in us as our Counselor, He will show us the rightness or wrongness of the decision. *Does my conscience confirm this decision?*
3. *The conviction test.* God will confirm the decision with a promise from His Word. It won't be just a nice verse, but a powerful promise that gives us confidence that this is the right decision. *Do I have a promise from God?*
4. *The counselor test.* We test the validity of the decision through the affirmation of people whose opinions we respect—spouse, parents, boss, or close friends. *Have those I respect confirmed the decision?*
5. *The calmness test.* We can picture ourselves carrying out the decision. Sleep on it. If the peace of Christ rules in your heart the next day (Col. 3:15), then move ahead. If not, reevaluate. *Do I have peace about the decision?*

When all five of these line up, you have thoroughly evaluated your decision and can move forward with even greater confidence than before.

Decisive question: Have I thoroughly evaluated this decision?

C. S. Lewis summarized how our decisions affect us: "Every time you make a choice, you are turning the central part of you that chooses into something a little different from what it was before. And taking your life as a whole with all of your innumerable choices, all your life long you are slowly turning this central thing either into a heavenly creature or a hellish creature."[3]

When Marcia, my friend, finishes weaving, she has a beautiful fabric, each piece unique according to the draft she set up. When we learn to place the yarn of our decisions on God's loom and then teach our teenagers to do the same, we can have confidence that He is weaving every decision according to His draft, His perfect plan for each of us.

Get Ready

1. Use the **DECIDE** approach to make one decision you face now. Process that through the sheet on page 158.
2. Talk through your decision with your spouse, friend, or teenager.
3. Cut out the wallet-sized card on page 158 and place it in your wallet so you can refer to it as you make other decisions.

Helping My Teenager Get Ready

1. Pray that God will give your teenager the desire and wisdom to make decisions that please Him. Pray specifically about one decision he or she is making now.
2. Work through the **DECIDE** approach on one decision with your teenager.
3. Show them a decision you made using the **DECIDE** approach.
4. Talk about what each of you is discovering in the process. Use the Funtalk questions.

Funtalk

1. What is your biggest hurdle in making decisions?
2. Let's go over one decision you made using the **DECIDE** approach. Let me tell you one decision I made using this approach.
3. How do you think this approach will help you in making future decisions?
4. Let's pray for each other about one major decision each of us needs to make.

Note: After you pray, clip out the wallet-sized card on page 158 and put it in your wallet.

Parents' Discussion Group

1. Have everyone make a list of the top ten decisions they have made since they left home that day.
2. Ask several people to walk all the way through a decision they made using the **DECIDE** approach.
3. Brainstorm ideas on how to help your teenagers make wise decisions. Talk about how they are doing in their decision-making process. Do this in smaller groups if you need to save time.
4. Pray for your teenager by name asking God to give him or her a deep desire to please God in every decision. Ask the Lord to give your teenager wisdom to make right decisions. Pray for his or her future spouse, college, and career.

DECIDE

The Decision:

Discern Your Attitude. Will this decision serve me or serve Christ?
Exalt Jesus as Lord. Is this decision based on what Jesus desires?
Choose to Obey. Am I choosing to obey?
Implement the **STEPS** Am I using **STEPS** to think through the decision?

> **S**ee the goal clearly.
> **T**ake in the facts.
> **E**valuate the alternatives.
> **P**roject strengths and weaknesses.
> **S**elect the best alternative.

Delight in the decision. Am I enjoying this decision?
Evaluate with tests. Have I thoroughly evaluated this decision?

> **C**ommunication test (listen intently)
> **C**onscience test (Holy Spirit confirmation)
> **C**onviction test (promise from God)
> **C**ounselor test (someone I respect)
> **C**almness test (peace)

DECIDE
The Decision:
Discern Your Attitude. Will this decision serve me or serve Christ?
Exalt Jesus as Lord. Is this decision based on what Jesus desires?
Choose to Obey. Am I choosing to obey?
Implement the STEPS Am I using STEPS to think through the decision?
See the goal clearly.
Take in the facts .
Evaluate the alternatives.
Project strengths and weaknesses.
Select the best alternative.
Delight in the decision. Am I enjoying this decision?
Evaluate with tests. Have I thoroughly evaluated this decision?
Communication test (listen intently)
Conscience test (Holy Spirit confirmation)
Conviction test (promise from God)
Counselor test (someone I respect)
Calmness test (peace)

14 Put Together "The Visible Man"

What is integrity, and how can your teenager pursue it?

On those days when nothing else would keep the kids attention, my wife Carol would drag out "The Visible Man." Its description: "An exciting dimensional model of the human body." Open the box and out pops the skull, sternum, ribs, liver, heart, stomach, and intestines. In addition it was equipped with ears, fibula, tibia . . . you get the idea. The "exciting" part of "The Visible Man" was that someone got to put these parts together.

NOW THAT WE HAVE OPENED THE BOX and looked at the various aspects of discovering our destiny, we need to put all of the pieces together, to integrate them, so we can see the whole picture.

The word *integrity* gets tossed around a lot. These days who knows what it means? Integrity comes from the math word *integer,* a whole—all of the fractions add up to a whole number. Webster's Dictionary defines integrity as "(1) the quality or state of being complete; unbroken; whole; (2) unimpaired; perfect condition; sound; (3) sound moral principles; upright; honest; sincere."

"My parents are hypocrites," teenagers say. "Certainly there is no such thing as a perfect parent," we say. As an astute observer of teenagers for over thirty years, I can tell you without a doubt that the biggest struggle kids have with their parents centers around integrity. What hampers our ability to be parents with integrity? Let's look back at Webster's definition.

- "Unbroken"—a fractured background either through divorce, alcohol, abuse, or some other trauma impedes our parenting abilities.

- "Unimpaired"—stress and pressure that manifests itself as depression, anger, bitterness, and hatred impair us and keep us from being free to raise our teenagers God's way.
- "Sound moral principles"—the guilt of lust, affairs, premarital sex, and pornography makes us morally unsound and undermines our ability to be upright in raising our children.

Wherever we have come from in the past or wherever we are now, God wants to get us into "perfect condition." No matter how big or small our hypocrisy, all He asks from us is honesty. Our honest transparency will lead to integrity. And integrity in us as parents will create a model of integrity our teenagers can follow.

What will that model of integrity look like? In our search to discover our destiny we can have all of the parts of our lives identified, like we identified the parts of "The Visible Man." But all of the parts have to fit together. The fractions must add up to make the whole number. The parts of "The Visible Man" have to fit together for him to look like a man. In the same way we must add up the fractions—the parts—of our lives that we have discovered in this book about our destiny. We must fit them together to get the whole picture of who we are and what God has in mind for us and our teenagers.

Conclusion: a person with integrity is integrated; all parts of his or her life add up to the whole.

SHAPE UP!

In God's amazing creativity He made each one of us vastly different from all others. Our job is to shape up: to discover how to take all of these different parts and shape them into our unique destiny.

Job acknowledged to God: "Your hands shaped me and made me" (Job 10:8). Paul, the apostle, exhorts us: "What right do you have, a human being, to cross-examine God? The pot has no right to say to the potter: *Why did you make me this shape?* A potter can do what he likes with the clay!" (Rom. 9:20–21).

In another situation Paul wrote that "we are God's workmanship, created in Christ Jesus to do good works" (Eph. 2:10). "Workmanship" has the connotation of "a unique work of art." God has shaped us uniquely to do His "good works," which is our destiny.

That unique shape manifests itself in a variety of individuals throughout the Bible.

Joseph

- The gift of a multicolored coat showed the love of his father.
- Being thrown in a pit and sold as a slave revealed the hatred of his brothers.
- Resisting the sexual advances of Potiphar's wife deepened his convictions.
- Years in prison for doing nothing wrong built his character.
- His rise to be an official of Egypt expressed his leadership ability.

Years later, reflecting on what his brothers had done, Joseph could see how God had shaped him. He said, "You intended to harm me, but God intended it for good to accomplish what is now being done, the saving of many lives" (Gen. 50:20).

God shaped him into a man capable of saving not only his family but his nation.

Moses

- A man of privilege raised in Pharaoh's household for forty years.
- A man God sent into the desert for forty years.
- God spoke to Moses in a burning bush.

When Moses complained that he had nothing to offer, what did the Lord say to him about his shape in Exodus 4:10–12? "Moses said to the Lord, 'O Lord, I have never been eloquent, neither in the past nor since you have spoken to your servant. I am slow of speech and tongue.' The Lord said to him, 'Who gave man his mouth? Who makes him deaf or mute? Who gives him sight or makes him blind? Is it not I, the Lord? Now go; I will help you speak and will teach you what to say.'"

God shaped him uniquely to lead the Israelites out of Egypt.

David

- The youngest son, he was sent by his dad to tend the sheep while his brothers went to war.
- Out in the fields with the sheep, he experienced God's presence and power.
- God anointed him to be king at an early age.
- A fierce warrior, he killed Goliath.
- Chased by King Saul, David lived in caves for several years.

In all of these experiences, what one main quality did God look for to determine the shape of David's life? "The Lord has sought out a man after his own heart and appointed him leader of his people" (1 Sam. 13:14). Later God used him to shape the destiny of a nation.

Esther

- A devout Jew, she was also a beautiful woman.
- She caught the eye of the king and became queen.
- As queen she found herself in the unusual position of being the only person who could appeal to the king not to destroy her people.

What profound challenge did her Uncle Mordecai give her regarding her shape in Esther 4:14? "For if you remain silent at this time, relief and deliverance for the Jews will arise from another place, but you and your father's family will perish. And who knows but that you have come to royal position for such a time as this?" Esther's grace under pressure shaped her destiny and that of the entire Jewish nation.

Job

- Early in his life he discovered success in all he did.
- Bombarded with Satan's entire arsenal, everything around him fell apart.
- He lost his work, friends, possessions, family, and health.

In spite of it all Job refused to toss in the towel. In Job 27:5 he revealed what kept him going, "Till I die, I will not deny my integrity." His integrity, based on absolute trust in God, led him to live out his unique destiny.

Up, Up and Away!

No less than any of these famous Bible characters, God has uniquely shaped each of us to achieve His destiny for us. But we short-circuit that when we think negatively:

- "God could never use me like that."
- "My life can't make much difference."
- "Only 'the rich and the famous' influence the world."

Yet if we faithfully pursue our destiny, God will use our humble lives to make a difference for His purposes.

> How can man now jet around the world and even fly to the moon? Air and space travel had a humble beginning. In 1670, an Italian monk, Francesco de Lana, developed a vacuum balloon that supported a cart equipped with oars and a sail. His flight experiment failed because he overlooked the phenomenon of atmospheric pressure, which crushed the balloon. Years later the Montgolfier brothers, inspired by Francesco de Lana and watching wood chips float over a fire, lifted a balloon six thousand feet in the air. They repeated the experiment for King Louis XVI with a sheep, rooster, and duck as the balloon's passengers. From that Henri Giffard flew a dirigible powered by a steam engine and propeller. Then the Wright brothers flew at Kitty Hawk . . . and now people explore space.

Humble beginnings, seemingly insignificant events, mostly unknown individuals laid the foundation for the next step. Each one had skeptics. Certainly they even doubted themselves at times. They must have asked the question: "Can it be done?" But they pursued their hopes and dreams, their unique destiny, and did it.[1]

When we pursue God's unique destiny, we can change the question, "Can it be done?" into a statement, "It can be done!"

All Put Together

In conclusion, we want to add all the fractions of our lives discovered in this book. When we do, we will be 80 percent of the distance in knowing our destiny. The other 20 percent, which has to do with whether or not we marry, who our marriage partner might be, and what our careers will look like, becomes clear as we pursue the 80 percent.

To bring us full circle, Jesus Christ is the one who puts all of the various parts together to make us complete. The apostle Paul said, "Your own completeness is only realized in him" (Col. 2:10).

No one else can do it. In Him all the parts come together into the whole.

How do we work that out in our daily lives? We do what Paul tells us in Colossians 2:6–7: "So then, just as you received Christ Jesus as Lord, continue to live in him, rooted and built up in him, strengthened in the faith as you were taught, and overflowing with thankfulness."

To "continue" indicates a process. We have developed a life plan in this book that we can live by every day for the rest of our lives. It has answered and will continue to answer these questions both for us and our teenagers:

1. What will be the center of my life?
   (Who or what am I going to live for?)
2. What will be the character of my life?
   (Who am I going to be?)
3. What will be the contribution of my life?
   (What strengths do I have?)
4. What will be the communication of my life?
   (What will God say to the world through me?)[2]

As we continue to discover, for ourselves and with our teenagers, the various aspects of who we are, where we are going, and how we are going to get there, God will use our families to influence the world. According to each one's uniqueness, He will complete His destiny for us!

GET READY

1. Evaluate how integrated you are by filling in the **INTEGRITY QUESTIONS** at the end of this chapter.
2. To put together the whole picture of who you are, fill in **THE TOTAL PICTURE** at the end of this chapter.
3. Keep these in your Bible or notebook as a continual reminder of who you are, where you are going, and how you are going to get there.
4. Talk about these with your teenager.

HELPING MY TEENAGER GET READY

1. Pray for your teenager that God will reveal the "total picture" of who he or she is as a result of this chapter.
2. Work through the **INTEGRITY QUESTIONS** and **THE TOTAL PICTURE** with your teenager. Set aside thirty minutes each night to work on it together.
3. Talk about how to use what you have discovered by helping your teenager get plugged in to a place to serve. (The chapter in your teenager's book has several suggestions on how to do this.) Use the Funtalk questions.

Funtalk

1. Be honest with me. Do you see anything hypocritical in my attitudes or actions?
2. Let's look at each other's **INTEGRITY QUESTIONS** and see what we need to work on.
3. Share with me **THE TOTAL PICTURE** and summarize who you think you are, where you are going, and how you are going to get there. Let me do the same with you.
4. How can we take what we have learned and plug it in to a specific, practical way to serve.
5. Let's thank God for who He has made us and how wonderful He is to let us know so much about who we are. Let's ask Him to make us people of integrity.

   Plan a celebration by going out to eat for this session or after it is over. Have a party!

Parents' Discussion Group

(Make a life-size poster of a person. Give everyone cards and markers. Bring scotch tape.)

1. Write down all of the information you filled out on **THE TOTAL PICTURE**. Put one piece of information on each card. Write in large letters.
2. Each one in turn come up to the big poster and tape your cards on, telling us what is on each card as you tape it.
3. In groups of two share with each other the three areas you need to work on from the **INTEGRITY QUESTIONS**.
4. Pray for each other that you will be a person of integrity.

Note: Plan to have a big party at the end of the meeting!

INTEGRITY QUESTIONS

Rank where you are on a scale of 1–10 (1=lowest, 10-highest).

Personality—Am I using what I know about my personality to maximize my strengths and minimize my weaknesses?

1 2 3 4 5 6 7 8 9 10

Spiritual gifts—Am I using my spiritual gifts in a specific ministry?

1 2 3 4 5 6 7 8 9 10

Abilities—Am I using my abilities and experiences to build the kingdom of God?

1 2 3 4 5 6 7 8 9 10

Motives—Am I motivated toward investing my life in God's plans and purposes?

1 2 3 4 5 6 7 8 9 10

Purpose—Do I know my purpose and am I pursuing it?

1 2 3 4 5 6 7 8 9 10

Values—Are my values determining my behavior?

1 2 3 4 5 6 7 8 9 10

Goals—Am I pursuing my long- and short-term goals?

1 2 3 4 5 6 7 8 9 10

Time—Am I using my time to pursue God's purpose and goals for my life?

1 2 3 4 5 6 7 8 9 10

Decisions—Am I making daily decisions that keep me in line with God's plan for me?

1 2 3 4 5 6 7 8 9 10

From the evaluation take the three lowest scores and decide what you need to do to integrate those more into your daily life.

1. ______________________________

2. ______________________________

3. ______________________________

THE TOTAL PICTURE

Put together the total picture of who you are, where you are going, and how you are going to get there. In order to do this you may need to review "Get Ready" in each of the chapters. Make your picture as clear and concise as you possibly can.

My destiny: ______________________
My purpose: ______________________
My personality: ______________________
My abilities and experiences:
1. ______________________
2. ______________________
3. ______________________
4. ______________________
5. ______________________

My values:
1. ______________________
2. ______________________
3. ______________________
4. ______________________
5. ______________________
6. ______________________

My motivation:
1. ______________________
2. ______________________
3. ______________________
4. ______________________
5. ______________________
6. ______________________

My goals:
1. ______________________
2. ______________________
3. ______________________
4. ______________________
5. ______________________

My time plan: ______________________
My decisions (ones to make in light of what I discovered):
1. ______________________
2. ______________________
3. ______________________

My destination: ______________________

THE TOTAL PICTURE

My destiny: ____________________

My purpose: ____________________

My personality: ____________________

My values:

My abilities & experience:

My goals:

My motivation:

My big decisions:

My time plan:

My destination: ____________________

Appendix

PARENTAL PERSONALITY TENDENCIES

	Strengths	Weaknesses
Doer		
	• exerts sound leadership	• tends to overdominate
	• establishes goals	• too busy for family
	• motivates family to action	• gives answer too quickly
	• knows the right answer	• impatient with poor performance
	• organizes household	• won't let children relax
Influencer		
	• makes home fun	• keeps home in a frenzy
	• liked by children's friends	• forgets children's appointments & activities
	• turns disaster into humor	• disorganized
	• circus master!	• doesn't listen to entire story
Relater		
	• good parent	• lax on discipline
	• takes time for children	• doesn't organize home
	• not in a hurry	
	• can take good with the bad	
	• doesn't get upset easily	
Thinker		
	• sets high standards	• puts goals beyond reach
	• wants everything done right	• may discourage children
	• picks up after children	• sometimes instills "guilt trip"[1]

PARENTING WITH PERSONALITY

THE INFLUENCER PARENT

No worse punishment exists than to be ignored by the family. Quiet treatment is deadly. Tells entertaining stories even if the truth is stretched.

With a Doer Child

- Parent will brag about children's accomplishments and achievement.
- Problem comes when child controls parent.

With an Influencer Child

- As long as there is no competition among them, life is fun.
- The teen years can present the greatest period for this competition.
- Mutual sense of humor, zeal for life.

With a Relater Child

- Influencer parent lives for excitement, but the relater child tends to avoid it.
- Parent loves noise and confusion (within reason); child avoids it because it threatens security and stability.

With a Thinker Child

- Child usually doesn't appreciate parent's humor; could be easily hurt by flippant comments meant to be funny.
- Opposite concepts of time.

THE DOER PARENT

Believes that if everyone would do everything his or her way *now*, we would all live happily ever after. Home is usually fast-paced and businesslike.

With a Doer Child

- Alternatives:
  (1) mutual goals: happiness
  (2) constant friction and fighting . . . WIN!
  (3) Eventually one gives up

With a Influencer Child

- Child can con parent, sometimes because of charm or acting.
- Knows what parent wants; can play parents off of each other to get desired results.

With a Relater Child

- Great natural blend. Parent-leader, submissive child.
- Avoid placing child in competitive situations unless the child wants it.

With a Thinker Child

- Challenge: to motivate without crushing; need to tone down
- Speak softly, but don't carry a big stick.

The Relater Parent

Has a kind, low-keyed, relaxed, patient, and sympathetic nature.

With a Doer Child

- The issue is control. Don't let the child control you or the family.

With a Influencer Child

- A good combination. Influencers thrive on response. Relaters respond well.

With a Relater Child

- Super combination! Both laid back and non-conflictual.

The Thinker Parent

Takes great pains to raise perfect kids!

With a Doer Child

- The issue is control. The child wants to control and lead. Keep on the same side with motivating challenges. Show appreciation for their efforts.

With an Influencer Child

- Possible trouble combination: opposites in regards to time, neatness, and so forth.
- Child may resort to rebellion to get attention.

With a Relater Child

- Low-key, reticent relationship.
- Child needs great encouragement.

With a Thinker Child

- Be careful of performance-based acceptance with your child.[2]

BIBLICAL PERSONALITY PROFILES

Choleric Paul

Probably the apostle Paul had a choleric personality. In Acts 9 he was on a crusade to wipe out all Christians (v. 1). Intensely he went after them, asking for official letters to throw them into prison (v. 2). Operating with no compassion whatsoever, he was going to get the job done and win at all costs.

The Lord had to use the dramatic event on the Damascus Road to get his attention. He was so determined to carry out his project, he never would have listened otherwise. The Lord blinded him to get him to slow down and listen. When he did follow Christ, he did so with radical, decisive intensity.

As fiercely as he had been against Christians before, he was fiercely for them after his conversion. Immediately he stepped into leadership. In just a few days, he was preaching in the synagogues. From that point on, his course was set. He had a cause. He boldly spoke for Christ and didn't let anything stand in his way, even the threat of death (9:28–29). God gave Paul a vision, a goal to achieve—to take the gospel to the Gentiles. Nothing was going to keep him from accomplishing that—not shipwreck, beatings, or prison.

Yet the other side of that "world-beater" personality found him quite unsympathetic to John Mark. He was so sure that John Mark was not dependable that he split with Barnabas over it. He had confrontations with the Council at Jerusalem (Acts 15) and with Peter (Gal. 2:11–21). He could be sarcastic and he could brag (2 Cor. 11:16–29).

Because of his personality, Paul knew that he needed to be "crucified with Christ" (Gal. 2:20) daily so he would not rely on himself or hinder his ministry by the weaknesses of his personality. As he did that, God unleashed his choleric personality to reach the entire known world for Christ.

Sanguine Simon Peter

Probably Simon Peter had the personality of a sanguine. Remember the transfiguration when Moses and Elijah appeared with Jesus? As soon as Peter saw them, what did he do? He talked: "Lord, this is terrific. Let's stay up here, pitch a tent, and camp out" (see Matt. 17:1–8).

Later Jesus asked His disciples who people were saying He is. Peter was the first to speak up: "You are the Christ." Then when Jesus told them He was going to die, Peter the promoter made a pitch for his program. "Jesus, now listen to old Peter. You are not going to die." Jesus silenced him and then put him in his place (see Matt. 16:13–20).

Or take the time Jesus washed the disciples' feet. Everyone else was very quiet, except Peter: "You're not going to wash my feet, Jesus." When Jesus told him that he would not be included if He didn't, Peter said, "Wash my hands and head as well." He couldn't stand the thought of not being included (John 13:1–8).

After Peter's personality was broken and humbled by his denial of Jesus, God powerfully used that same ability to talk to people to convert three thousand people at Pentecost (Acts 2:13–41). The Holy Spirit transformed Peter's sanguine temperament. Under the control of Christ, Peter's personality was used mightily by God.

Phlegmatic Nathaniel

Most likely, Nathaniel (Bartholomew), had a phlegmatic personality. He probably would not have taken the initiative to go and meet Jesus if Philip had not persuaded him (John 1:44–47). Then Jesus took the initiative to draw Nathaniel into a conversation (v. 47). Jesus complimented and appreciated him: "Here is a true Israelite, in whom there is nothing false." Jesus praised him for having no hidden agendas or wrong motives, for being consistent and balanced.

Jesus spoke about the vision of what God was doing and showed Nathaniel his role in that (John 1:50–52). Nathaniel needed that encouragement to get involved. Once he did, he became a faithful, steady, and consistent disciple. He never asserted himself like Peter did, yet he is there, supporting Jesus all the way through the cross and resurrection (John 21:1–4). He is there again after the resurrection, quietly dependable, low-key, and supportive. Filled with the Holy Spirit, he offered well-balanced leadership to the early church.

Melancholy John the Baptist

The probability exists that John the Baptist had a melancholy personality. Because he lived in the wilderness, we could say he was withdrawn in his lifestyle. His creativity and imagination fit the profile of an artist, as did his weird clothes and unconventional eating habits! So honed was his message of repentance that it came from his mouth with the accuracy and precision of a laser (Mark 1:2–8). He preached it with emotion, calling the religious leaders "snakes" and "whitewashed fences."

A man of humility, he always played second fiddle to Jesus. He said, "I must decrease, so that He might increase" (John 3:30). As Jesus' loyal friend, he wound up going to prison, and eventually dying, for that friendship (Matt. 11:2–6).

In prison he got depressed. A perfectionist, he had all the details of Jesus' ministry worked out. When Jesus didn't follow the script, John began to doubt (Luke 7:18–23). John denied himself, endured in prison, and suffered martyrdom for his friend Jesus (Matt. 14:1–12).

When John the Melancholy Baptist lived in the energy of the Holy Spirit, he gained the title as the greatest man who ever lived. (Eat your heart out Muhammad Ali.) Jesus Himself gave John that title (Luke 1:41; Matt. 11:11).

Notes

Chapter 2

1. William Barclay, "The Letter to the Galatians and Ephesians," *The Daily Study Bible,* 88–89.

Chapter 3

1. Ibid., 101–102.
2. Peter Marshall Jr. and David Manuel, *The Light and the Glory* (Grand Rapids, Mich.: Fleming H. Revell Co., 1977), 17.

Chapter 4

1. Larry Crabb, *Inside Out* (Colorado Springs, Colo.: NavPress, 1988), 80–81.

Chapter 5

1. Tim LaHaye, *Spirit-Controlled Temperament* (Wheaton, Ill.: Tyndale House, 1966), 10.
2. Information on these personality types came from a variety of sources including Tim LaHaye, *Spirit-Controlled Temperament,* Fred and Florence Littauer, "Personality Plus" (Redlands, Calif.), Forrest and Nancy Mobley, "Marriage Lifelines" notebook based on the DISC test (Tallassee, Ala.:), and my personal observations.
3. The instructions, test, and scoring sheet were developed for me by Bill Kallenburg of Student Leadership Development (Avondale Estates, Ga.), used with permission.

Chapter 6

1. Barry St. Clair, "Gifted Supernaturally," *Influencing Your World* (Wheaton, Ill.: Victor Books, 1991), 58–69.
2. This material was developed by Don Crossland and used by Bill Gothard in his institute and Basic Youth Conflicts notebook. It was adapted by Don Dunlap and then I adapted it again.

Chapter 7

1. "Discovering my S.H.A.P.E. for Ministry," Ft. Worth, Tex., Hope Baptist Church, 34.
2. Dennis Rainey, *Soapbox* newsletter (Little Rock, Ark., 1986).
3. The Abilities Survey is adapted from an abilities test in "Discovering My S.H.A.P.E. for Ministry," Hope Baptist Church, Ft. Worth, Tex., 35–36.
4. Ibid., 30–31.

Chapter 8

1. Alan Loy McGinnis, *Bringing Out the Best in People* (Minneapolis, Minn.: Augsburg, 1985), 15.
2. These topics taken from Jesus in Mark 4:19.

Chapter 9

1. Quoted from Billy Graham, *World Aflame* (Garden City, N.Y.: Doubleday, 1965). 67.
2. Ibid., 64.
3. Walter A. Henrichsen, *Disciples Are Made, Not Born* (Wheaton, Ill.: Scripture Press, 1988), 150.
4. Mack R. Douglas, *How to Make a Habit of Succeeding* (Grand Rapids: Zondervan Publishing House, 1966), 19.

Chapter 10

1. Allan Bloom, *The Closing of the American Mind* (New York: Simon and Schuster, 1987), 25.
2. Richard Halverson, "Perspective," vol. 27, no. 1 (8 January 1975).
3. Charles Hobbs, "Your Time and Your Life" tape series and workbook, Charles R. Hobbs Corporation, 7300 N. Leheigh Ave., Chicago, Ill. 60648).
4. T. B. Maston and William Pinson Jr., *Right from Wrong?* (Nashville: Broadman Press, 1971), 15–20.

Chapter 11

1. Mike Philips, *Getting More Done in Less Time* (Minneapolis, Minn.: Bethany House Publishers, 1982), 55.
2. Ari Kiev, *A Strategy for Daily Living* (New York: The Free Press, a division of Simon & Schuster, 1973), 3.
3. Several ideas that follow came from Wilberta L. Chinn, *Personal Goal Setting for a Purposeful and Fulfilled Life* (Whittier, Calif.: Peacock Enterprises, 1984).
4. Charles Hummel, *Tyranny of the Urgent* (Downers Grove, Ill.: InterVarsity Press, 1967), 5.
5. Glenn Bland, *Success! The Glenn Bland Method* (Wheaton, Ill.: Tyndale, 1972), 44.

6. Mack Douglas, *How to Make a Habit of Succeeding* (Grand Rapids: Zondervan Publishing House, 1966), 49.
7. David Schwartz, *The Magic of Thinking Big* (New York: Prentice-Hall, 1990 n. p. Quoted in Howard Hendricks, *Heaven Help the Home* (Wheaton, Ill.: Scripture Press, 1990).

Chapter 12

1. Edward R. Dayton and Ted W. Engstrom, *Strategy for Living* (Oxnard, Calif.: Gospel Light Publishing, 1976).
2. William M. Elliot, *For the Living of These Days,* ed. C. Michael Hawn (Macon, Ga.: Smyth & Helwys, 1995).
3. The Charles Hobbs, "Your Time and Your Life" tape series, (Chicago, Ill.: Nightingale-Conant Corporation), and Edward R. Dayton, *Tools for Time Management* (Grand Rapids: Zondervan Publishing House), 176.
4. Quoted in Dayton and Engstrom, *Strategy for Living,* 177.
5. Mike Philips, *Getting More Done in Less Time* (Minneapolis, Minn.: Bethany House Publishers), 35.
6. Howard Hendricks, "Managing Time" tape, (Ventura, Calif.: Vision House Publishers, 1974) as quoted in Wilberta Chinn, *Personal Goal Setting,* 35.
7. Les Christie, *Getting a Grip on Time Management* (Wheaton, Ill.: Victor Books, 1984), 32.
8. Quoted in Christie, 32.

Chapter 13

1. James Dobson, *Life on the Edge* (Dallas: Word Publishing, 1995), 3.
2. Myron Rush, *Management: A Biblical Approach* (Wheaton, Ill.: Victor Books, 1983), 102–106.
3. C. S. Lewis, *Christian Behavior* (New York: MacMillan, 1943), 23.

Chapter 14

1. Taken from a monthly newsletter published by Bill Kallenberg (Avondale Estates, Ga.)
2. Rick Warren and Tom Patterson, "Defining Your Life Mission" tape (Holland, Mich.: Authentic Leadership Inc.)

Appendix

1. Bill Kallenburg, "Student Leadership" seminar material (Avondale Estates, Ga.), used with permission.
2. Ibid.